Set design by Scott Bradley   *Photo by Jay Westhauser*

A scene from the Milwaukee Repertory Theater
production of *The Servant of Two Masters*.

Carlo Goldoni's
THE SERVANT OF TWO MASTERS

TRANSLATED AND ADAPTED BY
JEFFREY HATCHER
AND
PAOLO EMILIO LANDI

★

★

DRAMATISTS
PLAY SERVICE
INC.

THE SERVANT OF TWO MASTERS
Copyright © 2004, Jeffrey Hatcher and Paolo Emilio Landi

All Rights Reserved

SPECIAL NOTE

AUTHOR'S NOTE

Framing Device

My co-adapter, the director Paolo E. Landi, devised the framing device for this adaptation. It concerns a band of eighteenth-century traveling players arriving in a small Italian village to put on a show — Carlo Goldoni's comedy *The Servant of Two Masters* — and a good deal of stage time is devoted to their arrival, their setup, their negotiations with a financial patron and their personal travails. Most important to this framing device is the illness of the comedian who plays Truffaldino, the servant of the title. During the show, we track the comedian's worsening condition, and at the end of the play when Truffaldino has finally emerged from his farcical adventures victorious ... the comedian dies.

This all worked very well in the Milwaukee Rep premiere, especially with the gifted Lee Ernst as The Comedian/Truffaldino. The pathos played off the comic proceedings and leant the show a wonderful resonance. And the comic framing scenes — an audience participation quiz to see if spectators were following the plot, a cast member who appeared with a sign reading "Exposition" whenever the back-story required special attention, a live duck, a "commercial" for the patron's new patent medicine near the top of Act Two, and various Milwaukee–specific ad-libs — were a huge hit with the audience.

However. We can imagine some theatres wishing to stick to the play itself and doing away with this frame. If this is the case, inform DPS and permission will be granted.

Cast Size

We were fortunate in Milwaukee to have use of the Rep's internship program, and so the stage was filled with additional players. While useful, these extra bodies are not essential. The only small roles that must be filled are the Waiters who dash in and out with Truffaldino in the wild juggling scene at the end of Act One. But these roles could be doubled by some of the principals and need not be played by men.

3

Juggling

This is a very physical show. It's commedia, after all, with lots of *lazzi* (traditional commedia del arte comic bits). The only time actual juggling is required is in that end of Act One plate scene. Again, Lee Ernst surpassed himself, juggling plates with the Waiters and never dropping a bit of china. Every night he got a standing ovation on this scene, sending the audience out to intermission on an incredible "contact high." The scene is tough, but you can do it, and when you do, the audience will be yours.

—*Jeffrey Hatcher*

This adaptation of THE SERVANT OF TWO MASTERS opened at the Milwaukee Repertory Theater (Joseph Hanreddy, Artistic Director; Timothy J. Shields, Managing Director) in Milwaukee, Wisconsin, on February 24, 1999. It was directed by Paolo Emilio Landi; the set design was by Scott Bradley; and the costume design was by Santi Migneco. The cast was as follows:

PANTALONE	Peter Silbert
CLARICE	Deborah Staples
DR. LOMBARDI	Jim Baker
SILVIO	Brian Vaughn
BEATRICE	Tamara Scott
FLORINDO	Joe Lutton
BRIGHELLA	Torrey Hanson
SMERALDINA	Carolynne Warren
TRUFFALDINO	Lee E. Ernst
PATRON/PORTER	Robb Hurst
FIRST WAITER	Christopher Spott
STAGE MANAGER	Jeremy Woods
ENSEMBLE	Melissa Cannady
	Damon Dunay
	Sharon Golinski
	Kate McDermott
	Samantha Montgomery
	Thomas Rosenthal
	Aaron Simms

CHARACTERS

TRUFFALDINO
SILVIO
CLARICE
PANTALONE
LOMBARDI
BRIGHELLA
SMERALDINA
BEATRICE
FLORINDO
PORTER
FIRST WAITER
SECOND WAITER

PLACE

Venice.

TIME

The eighteenth century.

THE ACTORS IN THE TRAVELING PLAYERS COMPANY AND THE ROLES THEY PLAY

Leading Player .... PANTALONE
Leading Lady .... BEATRICE
Matinee Idol .... FLORINDO
Comic .... TRUFFALDINO
Character Man .... BRIGHELLA
Character Woman .... SMERALDINA
Patron .... PORTER
Male Ingénue .... SILVIO
Female Ingénue .... CLARICE
Supporting Player .... LOMBARDI
Stage Manager .... MUFFELETTA
Stage Hands .... WAITERS

6

THE SERVANT OF TWO MASTERS

ACT ONE

Prologue

Before the play starts, various "locals" fill the stage, waiting for the arrival of the players. One Young Woman has a duck or chicken she is leading on a leash. He is called "Mario" and she may use his name on occasion. Men and women flirt. A musician might strum an instrument. It's a lazy day. Then ... as the lights begin to go down ...

YOUNG WOMAN. Do you see them?

OTHERS. Yes, they're coming, they're coming! *(The players and musicians arrive with much fanfare. The leading player, who plays Pantalone, comes DSC.)*

PANTALONE. *(To audience.)* Ladies and gentlemen, a thousand mea culpas, our company was unavoidably detained. Traffic on the canal outside was not to be believed. We are about to perform for you Signor Goldoni's comedy *The Servant of Two Masters*, but we have a few minor details to finesse before the gaiety can begin, so we beg your patience and good graces. Sit back, relax ... and read the advertisements in your programs. Oh, stage manager!

STAGE MANAGER. *(Steps forward.)* Yes, sir?

PANTALONE. Disembark the stage from the barge!

STAGE MANAGER. Yes, sir! *(To others.)* All right, company, here the stage, here the properties table, and there the costumes. *(The locals help the actors construct a makeshift stage. The young girl exits, chasing after Mario. As the stage is "constructed," the actress playing Beatrice storms past, grumbling.)*

BEATRICE. I was told I could wear a beautiful gown! I only took this part because I was told I could wear a beautiful gown! *(Storms off.)*

STAGE MANAGER. Sir, we've lost the prompter!

PANTALONE. What?

STAGE MANAGER. We lost the prompter!

PANTALONE. Whaddaya mean, we LOST him? What happened?

STAGE MANAGER. He must've fallen out of the boat! That turn at the Bridge of Sighs was a doozy.

PANTALONE. Well, what'll we do if one of the actors forgets his lines? We've got to find a new prompter! Put up a sign! "PROMPTER WANTED." Whoever can read it gets the job!

STAGE MANAGER. Yes, sir! Oh, also the crew wants to be paid.

PANTALONE. We're trying to stage great art and they want to be paid?! We'll have to get an advance on the box office. *(Stage Manager and Pantalone exit. The actors who play Silvio and Clarice come by, running lines.)*

SILVIO. "Take this my hand and with it my heart." "Take this my hand and with it my heart." "Take this my hand and with it my heart —"

CLARICE. "Ingrate! That I should die and you not heave a single sigh! I shall die, and die of grief, and when I die, you'll get your wish and know that I was innocent. And it'll be too late, and you'll be the one crying then!" *(Silvio tries to take her hand. She slaps it away.)* Hey!

SILVIO. *(Backs away.)* I'm just trying to inhabit my part!

CLARICE. *(Pointed.)* Fine, just don't try to inhabit MY part. *(They exit. The actor who plays Truffaldino comes DSC. He is pale and coughs into a handkerchief. Pantalone comes down to him and speaks sotto voce.)*

PANTALONE. Is it any better? *(Truffaldino sighs.)* Yes. Well. Break a leg, eh? Oh, Signor Padrone? *(Truffaldino exits as the Patron enters. He carries a satchel.)*

PATRON. Signor Impresario!

PANTALONE. Signor Padrone, I cannot tell you how grateful we poor players are to you for providing us our food, our drink, our lodging, and per diem. Er, you don't happen to have the —

PATRON. What, the money? Right here in my satchel! *(Pats satchel.)*

PANTALONE. Perhaps you'd like to give it to our stage manager...? *(Stage Manager crosses in front of them.)*

PATRON. I'll keep my gold against my girth, thanks! No, what I am concerned about is my samples.

PANTALONE. Ah, yes. Most patrons set up a sort of "booth" for the audience to peruse during the intermission.

PATRON. I'm not setting up any booth! I intend to display my wares ONSTAGE! This is my newest patent! *(Takes a bottle of patent medicine out of his satchel.)* A natural elixir from the wilds of the Caribbe. It's called Fricandeau.
PANTALONE. What?
PATRON. Fricandeau.
PANTALONE. Frican — ?
PATRON. Fricandeau! Fricandeau!
PANTALONE. What's it mean?
PATRON. *(Angry.)* It means the difference between being paid and not being paid! I want you to advertise my Fricandeau during your show.
PANTALONE. *(Red-faced.)* You want us to HAWK a commercial product alongside bountiful verse and deathless prose?
PATRON. *(Pointed.)* No, I want you to do it during the play Now! What role am I to play?
PANTALONE. Role?
PATRON. I was told I would be able to play a part. Nothing big, mind you, just a featured cameo so that my wife, mother, children, in-laws, neighbors and business associates can see and take notice.
PANTALONE. *(To Stage Manager.)* Our respected patron shall play Floggolozzo the Porter.
STAGE MANAGER. But Floggolozzo the Porter is a skinny, old man who gets kicked in the — *(Pantalone smiles at him — turns to Patron.)* Yes. Floggolozzo. You were born to play it.
PANTALONE. Come, stage manager, let's find that new prompter! *(Pantalone and Stage Manager go off. The young woman who had Mario comes in. Mario is missing. She calls for him. The actor who plays Brighella enters. The Patron buttonholes him.)*
YOUNG WOMAN. Mario! MARIO!
PATRON. Hey, you. You wanna make money?
BRIGHELLA. No, I'm in the theater.
PATRON. *(Shows him gold coin.)* Say Fricandeau.
BRIGHELLA. What?
PATRON. Fricandeau.
BRIGHELLA. Fricandeau.
PATRON. *(Gives him coin.)* Terrific. Slip it in whenever you can. *(The actress who plays Smeraldina enters.)*
BRIGHELLA. *(Eyeing Smeraldina.)* I do. *(Patron smiles and exits. Brighella buttonholes the Stage Manager.)* Hey, you seen…? *(Meaning Truffaldino.)*

STAGE MANAGER. He's over there. *(They turn to see Truffaldino off at the side of the stage, putting on makeup.)*
BRIGHELLA. Still? *(Meaning still sick?)*
STAGE MANAGER. Still. *(Meaning yeah, he's very sick.)*
BRIGHELLA. He won't talk about it.
STAGE MANAGER. That's how he wants it. *(Pantalone enters. The stage is now ready.)* Pantalone, I found our new prompter!
PANTALONE. Terrific! It's almost time, call places!
STAGE MANAGER. Yes, sir! Two minutes, everyone! Two minutes to curtain! *(Beatrice begins to sing an Italian song. Someone strums an instrument. Truffaldino looks over at Beatrice. She is singing. His heart melts. Finally she stops singing and crosses in front of Truffaldino. He stands and a flower materializes in his hand. Truffaldino offers the flower to Beatrice. Beatrice looks slightly taken aback. Then the flower droops. It's a joke flower. Beatrice smiles and shakes her head at him. She exits. His smile drops. He looks at the flower. He kisses it and blows its "spores" towards her exit. Three loud bangs off. The actors scramble to get in place. Truffaldino puts on his mask. He exits.)*
YOUNG WOMAN. Mario! Mario!
STAGE MANAGER. Act One, Scene One! The house of Pantalone! *(The Young Woman dashes off. And the play begins ...)*

Scene 1

A room in the house of Pantalone.

ALL. *(Ad lib.)* Hooray! Huzzah! Happy day! This is so exciting! Look at them! They'll make quite a couple! I can hardly wait!
SILVIO. *(Offering his hand to Clarice.)* Take this my hand and with it my heart. *(Clarice stares at Silvio with dreamy eyes.)*
PANTALONE. Psst! Clarice! Your heart, hand it over! First the engagement, THEN the marriage.
CLARICE. Dearest Silvio. With this hand, I will thee hold, with this heart, I will thee love. With this love, I will thee wed.
SILVIO. Thy heart, thy hand, thou art my bride-to-be. *(They take hands.)*
DR. LOMBARDI. Now it's legal, and there's no turning back!

10

SMERALDINA. *(Aside.)* Lucky girl. What I wouldn't give to hold one of those!

PANTALONE. *(To Brighella and Smeraldina.)* You two, Smeraldina and Brighella, be witness to the formal engagement between my daughter Clarice and Signor Silvio, worthy offspring of my friend, the good Doctor Lombardi!

BRIGHELLA. It's an honor.

PANTALONE. Ah, Brighella, I was a witness at your wedding, and now here you are a witness at Clarice's. Since you're the innkeeper, I want you to make this wedding an intimate affair. I'm not one of those fathers of the bride who *invites* everybody in town just so he can *impress* everybody in town. I'm sure Doctor Lombardi agrees: a small dinner and reception with no extra bodies at the table. What do you say, children, does that sound good?

SILVIO. *(Re: Clarice.)* Sir, I desire no more nourishment than these delicacies laid out before me.

SMERALDINA. *(Aside.)* He's right, there's nothing better than getting laid ... out delicacies.

DR. LOMBARDI. Pantalone, my boy is a truth-teller, and truth be told, he loves that little girl of yours more than heaven itself!

PANTALONE. Yes, it's a match made in Heaven ... because if Heaven hadn't preemptively beckoned my daughter's first fiancé, my business associate Federigo Rasponi, I could not now bestow her hand upon your son.

SILVIO. Yes, Signor Rasponi's untimely death came just in time, wouldn't you agree, Clarice?

CLARICE. Silvio, I was prepared to give Signor Rasponi my hand, but only because my dear, good father had so decreed. Whatever flesh he might have held, my heart would have been yours.

DR. LOMBARDI. Verily, Heaven works in mysterious ways. Say, how did Rasponi die anyway?

PANTALONE. The poor fellow was slain. A scandal involving his sister. He was stabbed to death and died on the spot.

BRIGHELLA. In Turin wasn't it?

PANTALONE. Yes.

BRIGHELLA. Alas, poor Rasponi. I knew him a little bit.

PANTALONE. You did?

BRIGHELLA. Three years I lived in Turin. Knew his sister too. Dressed like a man, rode like a man. But her brother loved her, and, well ... *(Tsks.)* ... No one escapes death, eh?

PANTALONE. *(Solemn and grim.)* True, true, death comes for us all ... *(Claps hands.)* — Okay, now that we're finished with the exposition, let's plan that wedding! *(A knock at the door.)* What's that, a knock? Smeraldina, see who it is.

SMERALDINA. Yes, sir. *(Goes to the door. Smeraldina brings in Truffaldino.)*

TRUFFALDINO. My most humble greetings, ladies and gentlemen, gentlemen and ladies. Why, what a fine, fine group, yes, yes, yes. Very fine, very fine, indeed.

PANTALONE. Who are you and what is your business?

TRUFFALDINO. *(To Pantalone, pointing to Clarice.)* Say, tell me, who's the ripe, juicy, succulent lady?

PANTALONE. My daughter.

TRUFFALDINO. *(Gulps.)* My congratulations.

SMERALDINA. *(Re: Silvio.)* And this is her fiancé.

TRUFFALDINO. My condolences. *(To Smeraldina.)* And who are you?

SMERALDINA. The lady's maid.

TRUFFALDINO. Lucky lady.

PANTALONE. All right, enough small talk. What do you want? Who are you? Who sent you?

TRUFFALDINO. Hey, three questions at once? Give a poor guy a chance.

PANTALONE. *(To Dr. Lombardi.)* Is it him or is it me?

DR. LOMBARDI. I think it's him.

TRUFFALDINO. *(To Smeraldina.)* So are you the one getting married?

SMERALDINA. *(Sighs.)* No.

PANTALONE. Look, tell me who you are or go about your business!

TRUFFALDINO. Well, if that's all you care about, FINE, I'll tell you in two words: I AM A SERVANT OF MY MASTER. *(Turns to Smeraldina.)* As I was saying —

PANTALONE. So who is your master!?

TRUFFALDINO. A gentleman from abroad who wants to have a word with you. *(To Smeraldina.)* So —

PANTALONE. WHAT GENTLEMAN?! WHAT IS HIS NAME?!

TRUFFALDINO. All right, long story short: My master is Signor Federigo Rasponi.

ALL. AHH, Federigo Rasponi!

TRUFFALDINO. He sends his regards. And he's come to see you. And he's downstairs. And he's ... WAITING! *(All look surprised. To*

Smeraldina, as before:) One more time —

PANTALONE. ... Uh, sir? Sir? Yes, you. Listen to me. WHAT THE HELL ARE YOU TALKING ABOUT?!

TRUFFALDINO. Hey, hey! If you want to know so bad, I am Truffaldino Battocchio from Bergamo.

PANTALONE. I don't care who you are. I mean your master! I didn't quite catch the name.

TRUFFALDINO. *(Aside.)* Poor guy ... deaf as cheddar. *(To Pantalone.)* My master is Signor Federigo Rasponi.

PANTALONE. But Federigo Rasponi of Turin is dead.

TRUFFALDINO. Dead?

PANTALONE. DEAD!

BRIGHELLA. Dead.

DR. LOMBARDI. Dead.

CLARICE. Dead.

SILVIO. Dead.

SMERALDINA. Dead.

ALL. DEAD!

TRUFFALDINO. Well, gotta go!

PANTALONE. Go? Wait a minute — !

TRUFFALDINO. Why? Dead's dead, he's not cheese, he's won't improve with age. *(Aside.)* Still, I should take a look myself. *(Exit.)*

PANTALONE. Well, what is he? A con man or an idiot?

DR. LOMBARDI. I think he's an idiot con man.

SMERALDINA. *(Aside.)* I don't think he's an idiot. I like him. He's swarthy. 'Scuse me sir, be right back! *(Runs off.)*

PANTALONE. But what about all this Rasponi business?

CLARICE. Father, if Signor Rasponi is alive I'm not going to be very happy.

PANTALONE. But you saw the death notice we received from Turin.

SILVIO. Well, we don't want him dead OR alive! We'll just tell him he's too late! *(Enter Beatrice, dressed as a man.)*

BEATRICE. Signor Pantalone, the kindnesses to which I had become accustomed via our friendly albeit faceless correspondence is, I fear, ill-matched by the treatment to which I have been subjected today. Having sent my servant to you, I had hoped for, nay expected, a quick and eager welcoming response, only to find I had been relegated to the street below for fully half an hour!

PANTALONE. *(Nervously.)* Beg pardon but ... who ARE you?

BEATRICE. Federigo Rasponi.

ALL. AHHH!

BRIGHELLA. *(Aside.)* WHAT'S THIS? That fellow isn't Federigo Rasponi. That's his sister Beatrice. And in disguise! Let's watch!

PANTALONE. I'm, er, happy to see you alive and well, Federigo Rasponi! And after we had heard ... otherwise. *(Aside to Dr. Lombardi.)* Keep calm! This Rasponi's a phoney!

BEATRICE. The story went I suffered a mortal wound in an affair of honor, but thanks to Heaven, the mortal wound was but a fleshy one, and once I was up and on my feet, it was on to Venice!

PANTALONE. Sir, I don't know how to say this, but I was promised Signor Rasponi was dead, so I know you'll understand when I say that we might require some small piece of evidence that would serve as proof to the contrary.

BEATRICE. I fully understand. Let me assuage your concerns as regards to my identity. Allow me to present these four letters from mutual acquaintances and associates, one of them your own banker. *(Gives four letters to Pantalone.)* I hope these suffice to satisfy you as to who I am. *(Noticing Brighella, aside.)* GASP! Brighella! What's he doing here? If he opens his mouth and tells them —

CLARICE. Silvio, our bright future is receding into the dark past!

SILVIO. Phooey, I'll not forfeit one fleck of thy flesh!

BEATRICE. *(Aloud to Brighella.)* Why, Good Sir, don't I know you?

BRIGHELLA. Yes, I think you do indeed. Brighella Cavicchio from Turin?

BEATRICE. Brighella! Yes, of course! Whatever brings you to Venice, my good and LOYAL friend? *(Aside to Brighella.)* Brighella! Don't spill the beans! — *(She hands him coins.)*

BRIGHELLA. *(Aside to Beatrice.)* Your secret's safe. *(Aloud.)* Why, sir, I run an inn.

BEATRICE. What a lucky coincidence: I need a room at an inn!

BRIGHELLA. Lucky you! I have an expensive one!

PANTALONE. Well, I've read the letters. They introduce the person who carries them as Signor Federigo Rasponi of Turin, and if you carry the letters introducing said person, then I must presume you are said person named therein.

BEATRICE. Don't believe me, believe good, loyal, HONEST Brighella; he knows me and can attest to my identity.

BRIGHELLA. Indeed, sir, this is a Rasponi if ever I saw one.

PANTALONE. Then given these letters and the fact that good Brighella confirms their contents, I can only say ... Welcome to

Venice, Signor Federigo, I'm sorry I ever doubted you.

CLARICE. You mean this really IS Rasponi? Silvio, we are lost! Grasp my shaking torso, lest I faint.

SILVIO. Fear not, my fiancée, this foppish foe shall not make thee a former!

BEATRICE. *(Pointing to Clarice.)* Er, Signor Pantalone, who is this fair creature?

PANTALONE. This is my daughter Clarice.

BEATRICE. The one I'm engaged to?

PANTALONE. Yes, sir; that's my baby.

BEATRICE. *(To Clarice.)* Madam, permit me.

CLARICE. *(Stiffly.)* Your servant, sir.

BEATRICE. *(To Pantalone.)* I see my fiancée is on the frosty side.

PANTALONE. She'll thaw come spring.

BEATRICE. *(Re: Silvio.)* And this is what, a poor relation?

PANTALONE. Nephew.

SILVIO. Sir, I am no nephew! I am the official fiancé of Signora Clarice!

DR. LOMBARDI. Get in there, boy! Stand up for your rights, but don't be rash! Only a fool rides off on a horse called "Anger."

BEATRICE. This pup is engaged to Signora Clarice? But Signora Clarice is engaged to me!

PANTALONE. This is easily explained. Dear Signor Federigo, we believed the story of your untimely demise was a true one, so Clarice got engaged to Silvio, but no harm done. I'm a man of my word, so here, take her, she's yours. Silvio, I don't know what to say. I'm sorry for your loss, but we do have some parting gifts for you.

SILVIO. Fie and enough! A gentleman would never take a bride who has given her hand to another.

BEATRICE. Oh, no, I would, I'll take her. *(Aside.)* Let's see what we can get away with here. *(Aloud.)* That is, unless Signora Clarice refuses my hand.

DR. LOMBARDI. Careful, son, only a fool rides a horse called "Hubris."

SILVIO. Sir! Signora Clarice is my fiancée, and there is nothing on earth that will make me yield her to you! Signor Pantalone, you do me wrong! And you, Signor Rasponi, if you presume to desire my heart's hand, you will have to fight for it against this, my large and long persuader. *(Draws sword, improvises swordplay.)*

DR. LOMBARDI. Sir, you have insulted the house of Lombardi and only a fool rides a horse called "Insult Dr. Lombardi." *(Dr.*

Lombardi and Silvio exit.)

BEATRICE. *(To Clarice.)* Well, my bride to be, what do you say?

CLARICE. You, sir, are a vile, rancid demon sent to torment me from the pits of hell! *(Clarice exits.)*

BEATRICE. She'll grow to love me. Meanwhile, let's get down to business. As you know, that is the OTHER reason that brings me here to Venice.

PANTALONE. Yes, sir. Your money is ready, and we'll settle our accounts soon as my clerk returns with the ledger book.

BEATRICE. Good. I'll come back when it's convenient.

PANTALONE. What's mine is yours! Er, figuratively. If you but need, you need but ask, but what needs one, who has so much?

BEATRICE. Well, I could use some walking around money. Didn't bring a penny with me. Afraid I'd be robbed along the way.

PANTALONE. The moment my clerk returns I'll send the money to Brighella's.

BEATRICE. Don't send it to me, let me send my servant to you. He's a very honest fellow, you can trust him with your life. Figuratively. *(Enter Smeraldina.)*

SMERALDINA. You're wanted downstairs, sir.

PANTALONE. Brighella, can you entertain my newest son-in-law while I — ?

BEATRICE. Please, don't trouble yourself.

PANTALONE. Oh, no, no trouble! No trouble! *(Aside.)* Please, God, no trouble! *(Exits with Smeraldina.)*

BRIGHELLA. So madam, let me ask you just one question —

BEATRICE. Quiet! You want everybody to hear?!

BRIGHELLA. As a matter of fact, yes! I've been rehearsing this play for five weeks and I still don't get the plot.

BEATRICE. This is what happened: My brother Federigo IS dead, killed by Florindo Aretusi, the only man I ever loved. 'Tis a tale of woe, and this is what transpired: Florindo Aretusi fell in love with me, but my brother Federigo forbade it. Federigo challenged Florindo, Florindo and Federigo fought, Federigo fell, Florindo fled, I followed Florindo. Now I'm Federigo, to whom Pantalone owed money, which, once I lay my hands on it, will help me find Florindo. Good, honest, loyal, discreet, HANDSOME Brighella, I beg you help me! You shall be justly rewarded.

BRIGHELLA. Oh, you little squash blossom. Turin lost a hellcat when you skipped town. Milady, you can rely on me, I will serve you as of old.

BEATRICE. Good! Now let's go to your inn. I told my servant to wait in the street.

BRIGHELLA. Say, where'd you find that guy? He don't even speak good.

BEATRICE. I picked him up on the road. He's not as stupid as he looks. By which I mean to say he's STUPID but not as stupid as he LOOKS. Still, he is loyal, and you can't buy that.

BRIGHELLA (*Looks at money she gave him.*) No, "loyalty"'s priceless. But "love." Ah, to think what love makes people do.

BEATRICE.
This is only the beginning.
"Love, say some, is like a song,
A verse let fly by Cupid,
But I know love can lead to wrong,
For Cupid makes us stupid."

(Beatrice and Brighella exit. Smeraldina enters.)

SMERALDINA. *(To audience.)* Hi. Hello. You know me as "Smeraldina, the innocent, impressionable lady's maid," but in real life, I'm an actress. We'll get back to the play in just one moment, but the management suspects many of you might not fully understand the plot at this point in the play, so I'm gonna give you a little quiz. Does this show take place in Sweden, Switzerland or Italy? *(Ad-lib as they banter, correct answer receives a mint candy.)* Okay, next question is a little easier. How many of you have eaten Italian food? Spaghetti? And how many of you really like anchovies? Okay, you probably need a mint. *(Gives a mint.)* Who was Clarice first engaged to? Was it Phil, Fred or Federigo? What happened to Federigo Rasponi back in Turin? *(Ad-lib during answers.)* Wonderful. Now to make sure you're listening to the very important exposition coming up in this next scene, we're going to have Muffeletta here ... *(She points to a beautiful girl who has just entered with a sign.)* come out here and focus your attention. *(The girl turns the sign. It reads: "Exposition.")* Thank you, Muffeletta. *(The girl curtsies and exits.)* One last question — what female character in the play do you find most winsome and attractive? Remember: My name is pronounced "Smer – al – dee – nah." *(Audience will probably yell back "Smeraldina." She throws mints and runs off.)* I love the theatre!

17

Scene 2

A street within Brighella's inn.

TRUFFALDINO. Waiting, waiting, waiting ... tongue dry, stomach empty ... My new master never has anything to eat, and the less there is the more I want. My other masters, first thing they did soon as they hit town was find a hotel and go to the bar. This one — NOOOO, this one leaves his luggage at the dock, traipses off to pay visits, forgets about his poor, starving servant. They tell us servants: "Serve your master with love." They should tell our masters, "Serve your servants some FOOD!" *(Enter Florindo in traveling dress with a Porter carrying a trunk on his shoulder.)*

PORTER. Sir, I beg you, I can't go any further; the weight's killing me!

FLORINDO. Yonder's the inn! Onward, man, it's just a few more steps.

PORTER. Help! The trunk, the trunk — !

FLORINDO. I told you you were too scrawny to carry it. A good servant needs meat on his bones! *(Florindo rearranges the trunk on the Porter's shoulder.)*

TRUFFALDINO. Here's my chance for the price of a lunch. *(To Florindo.)* Oh, sir? May I be of assistance?

FLORINDO. Good man! Carry this trunk into the inn there, would you?

TRUFFALDINO. Yes, sir, allow me, sir. *(Truffaldino puts his shoulder under the trunk and takes it by himself, knocking the Porter down at the same time.)*

FLORINDO. Bravo!

TRUFFALDINO. Light as a feather. *(Goes into the inn with the trunk.)*

FLORINDO. *(To Porter.)* There! See?

PORTER. *(Collapses.)* I'm done! I may be Floggolozzo, the porter, but that's only because I fell out of the middle class. I just thank the Lord my revered father is no longer alive to see how far I've fallen ... *(Weeps.)*

FLORINDO. Why, what did your father do?

18

PORTER. He was the village cretin.

FLORINDO. I see. *(Aside.)* Lunatic. *(To Porter.)* You may go. *(Going towards the inn.)*

PORTER. What about my pay?!

FLORINDO. You walked ten yards. The dock is right there.

PORTER. I'm not paid by the step. Pay me. *(Holds out his hand.)*

FLORINDO. Two pennies. *(Gives money.)*

PORTER. Pay me. *(Still holding out his hand.)*

FLORINDO. Two more. *(Gives money.)*

PORTER. Pay me.

FLORINDO. *(Kicks him.)* Get out of here!

PORTER. Paid in full! *(He exits.)*

FLORINDO. Eccentric little oddball. I think he wanted to be kicked. Well, let's see what this inn is like. *(Reenter Truffaldino.)*

TRUFFALDINO. Sir, your bags await.

FLORINDO. Good, good. Say, what sort of place is this, eh?

TRUFFALDINO. A good place, sir. Soft beds, clean glasses, big kitchen! And the smell! What they call "a comfort smell." I had a word with the waiter. You'll be served like a king.

FLORINDO. Top drawer. And what do YOU do?

TRUFFALDINO. Me? I'm a servant.

FLORINDO. From here in Venice?

TRUFFALDINO. Not Venice proper, but Greater Venice. Out state. Bergamo.

FLORINDO. You have a master now?

TRUFFALDINO. You know, to tell you the truth, at the moment I don't.

FLORINDO. No master?

TRUFFALDINO. Do you see a master? *(Aside.)* He's not here, I'm not lying.

FLORINDO. What say I hire you to be my servant?

TRUFFALDINO. Your servant! Why not? *(Aside.)* If the price was right, I'd work for his horse. *(Aloud.)* How much?

FLORINDO. How much do you want?

TRUFFALDINO. Well, my last master, the other one, the one who is no more, gave me a ducat a day and all I could eat.

FLORINDO. I can manage that.

TRUFFALDINO. Good, 'cause for you it's more.

FLORINDO. How much?

TRUFFALDINO. Ducat and a half.

FLORINDO. Done! Now I'm rather anxious to know if there are

19

any letters for me at the post office, so here *(Hands him coins.)* and ask if there's anything for Florindo Aretusi. If so, retrieve whatever is given to you and bring it back posthaste. I'll wait here.

TRUFFALDINO. And you'll order dinner, sir?

FLORINDO. Er … sure. Dinner it is! *(Aside.)* Funny fellow. But worth a shot, eh? *(Florindo goes into the inn.)*

TRUFFALDINO. A ducat and a half a day! That's a lot of money! Actually, my other master, that clueless, beardless boy from Turin, doesn't really pay a ducat a day. Who cares? He's history. I'm off to the post office for my new master! *(As he is going, Beatrice enters with Brighella and meets him.)*

BEATRICE. Oh, I see! This is how you wait for me?

TRUFFALDINO. Why — yes, sir! I am waiting for you, sir!

BEATRICE. Then why aren't you in the street like I told you? What was I supposed to do, meet you by accident?

TRUFFALDINO. I went for a stroll to walk off my appetite.

BEATRICE. Well, stroll to the docks; I want my trunk brought to the inn of Master Brighella.

TRUFFALDINO. Where's the inn?

BRIGHELLA. It's easy … *(Improvise directions to the inn using references that refer to local landmarks of the city in which the play is being performed.)*

BEATRICE. Hurry up, I'm waiting.

TRUFFALDINO. Just show me where it is!

BRIGHELLA. *(Points.)* Right there in front of you!

TRUFFALDINO. Damn! The same inn!

BEATRICE. And go down to the post office and see if there are any letters for me. Better yet, see if there are any letters for me or for my sister Beatrice Rasponi.

TRUFFALDINO. And then you'll order dinner, right? Huh…? *(Exit Brighella and Beatrice into the inn.)* I can't believe it! Some servants look for a master all their life, I've got two in the space of an minute. Now what am I gonna do? Wait on them both? No? Why not? Why can't I? It'd be twice the honor to work for two such fine masters and earn two such fine salaries. It'd be even better if neither found out about the other. And even if they did, what are they gonna do, fire me? I lose one job, I got the other. It shall be the test of skills I've always yearned for! Even if it's just a day, it'll be worth my every effort. *(Enter Silvio.)*

SILVIO. *(Aside.)* Hark! The servant of Federigo Rasponi!

TRUFFALDINO. And now off to the post office for my two masters!

SILVIO. Oh, domestic!

TRUFFALDINO. Sir?

SILVIO. Where is your master?

TRUFFALDINO. My master's inside the inn.

SILVIO. Tell him I wish a word. Tell him if he is a man of honor, he must come. Tell him I wait. Go.

TRUFFALDINO. Tell my master? Which mast —

SILVIO. *(Angrily.)* I said go!

TRUFFALDINO. But you have to understand, my masters —

SILVIO. I said go!

TRUFFALDINO. *(Aside.)* All right, I'll send the first one I find. *(Exit Truffaldino into the inn.)*

SILVIO. Yes! Bring forth my rival, he whose existence I shall not suffer! Federigo Rasponi may have escaped with his life once before, but he shan't be so lucky this time. Either he renounces his claim to Clarice, or I shall demand satisfaction. But wait! Footsteps from the inn. My plot needs privacy! To the periphery, fly! *(Enter Truffaldino with Florindo.)*

TRUFFALDINO. *(Points out Silvio.)* There he is, the beast.

FLORINDO. I don't know him. What's he want with me?

TRUFFALDINO. I don't know, I'm just trying to go to the post office. *(Exits.)*

FLORINDO. Sir, are you the gentleman who inquired after me?

SILVIO. I, sir? No, sir. I've not even had the honor of your acquaintance, sir.

FLORINDO. But my servant said that a man with a bellicose manner wanted to challenge me to a duel.

SILVIO. Must've been a misunderstanding. I said I wanted a word with his master.

FLORINDO. Well, that's me. I'm his master.

SILVIO. Then I beg your pardon, sir, but either your servant is identical to one I saw this morning, or he is servant to another master.

FLORINDO. No, I'm his, he's mine.

SILVIO. Huh. If that's so, I beg your pardon once again.

FLORINDO. 'S all right. Mistakes happen.

SILVIO. Er ... tell me, sir, are you by any chance a stranger to this city?

FLORINDO. I am a simple traveler from Turin.

SILVIO. Funny. The man whom I did so "bellicosely" challenge is from Turin as well.

FLORINDO. If he has insulted you, I shall gladly help you obtain satisfaction. What's his name?

SILVIO. His name? His name is … Federigo Rasponi.

FLORINDO. Ah! I knew him only too well.

SILVIO. He makes a claim of matrimony, based on an errant father's promise, to the fair lady whom this very morn swore to be my wife.

FLORINDO. The cad! Rest easy, friend, Federigo Rasponi cannot steal away your bride or any other's ever again. The man Rasponi … is dead.

SILVIO. Yes, well, that's what WE thought too. We ALL thought he was dead. But then this morning he showed up in Venice safe and sound.

FLORINDO. No!

SILVIO. Yes!

FLORINDO. Sir! Your news makes me shake!

SILVIO. You should have seen ME! I'm STILL shaking! Signor Pantalone dei Bisognosi, my fair fiancée's father, has made every inquiry. He holds in his hand incontestable proof that Rasponi is alive, in Venice, in person.

FLORINDO. (Aside.) So Federigo is alive, in Venice, in person? I fled from afar only to find in fleeing my foe!

SILVIO. If you see the vile villain, tell him that for his own safety he must abandon all hope of any legal coupling between himself and the lovely Clarice. By the way, if you ever need me my name is Lombardi. Silvio Vincent Lombardi. (Exit Silvio.)

FLORINDO. Nay, it cannot be! I stabbed him, stabbed him through and through, didst see him lying there before me, all … stabbed! Though I could swear my stab was true, it must have missed his shrunken heart! The fault is mine! Once accused of murder, I did not pause to look, but fled the scene as fast and as far as my steed could speed. But wait! If he's not dead, I must return to Turin and console my beloved Beatrice, who is more than likely suffering pangs of abject sorrow for the pain of my errant absence. Ah, Beatrice! (Truffaldino enters.)

TRUFFALDINO. DAMN! There's my other master.

FLORINDO. Truffaldino! Have you been to the post office?

TRUFFALDINO. I have, sir.

FLORINDO. Were there any letters for me?

TRUFFALDINO. There were, sir.

FLORINDO. Where are they?

TRUFFALDINO. Right here, sir. (Takes three letters out of his *pocket. Aside.)* DAMN! I've mixed them up. One master's letters mixed with the other master's letters mixed with the other's … I can't tell which is which. I CAN'T READ!

FLORINDO. Well? Come on, give me my letters.

TRUFFALDINO. Coming up! *(Aside.)* I think I've stepped in something. *(To Florindo.)* I must confess, sir: These three letters which I carry on me are not all for you. Y'see, a funny thing happened on the way to the post office, I met this servant I used to know in Bergamo; and I told him I was going to the post office, and this fellah, the other servant said, "Oh! Could you see if there's anything for my master." So, I said, sure, and sure enough there was one letter, but to tell you the truth, I don't know which one it is.

FLORINDO. Well, here, give me the stack. I'll find mine and give the rest back.

TRUFFALDINO. Thank you, sir; I only wanted to do a friend a good turn.

FLORINDO. *(Aside.)* Hang on! A letter addressed to Beatrice Rasponi? To Beatrice Rasponi at Venice?

TRUFFALDINO. Did you find the one that belongs to my friend's master — ?

FLORINDO. Who is this friend of yours and who asked you to do this for him?

TRUFFALDINO. Uh … well, as I said, he's a servant … name of … Pasquale —

FLORINDO. Who is his master?

TRUFFALDINO. I don't know, sir.

FLORINDO. But if he told you to pick up his master's letters, he must have told you his name.

TRUFFALDINO. Of course he did. *(Aside.)* Whatever I stepped in it's getting stickier.

FLORINDO. So what's his name?

TRUFFALDINO. I don't recall.

FLORINDO. What?

TRUFFALDINO. He wrote it down on a piece of paper.

FLORINDO. So where's the paper?

TRUFFALDINO. I left it at the post office.

FLORINDO. *(Aside.)* A confounding and mysterious complication!

TRUFFALDINO. *(Aside.)* Come on, I'm making this up as I go along.

FLORINDO. Where does Pasquale live?

TRUFFALDINO. I haven't the slightest idea.

FLORINDO. Well, if you don't know where he lives how are you going to give him the letter?

TRUFFALDINO. Good question! And the answer is—he said he'd meet me in the plaza.

FLORINDO. *(Aside.)* More mystery.

TRUFFALDINO. *(Aside.)* If I get out of this, I'm going into politics. *(To Florindo.)* Tell you what, sir, give me the letter and I promise to make sure he gets it.

FLORINDO. Not a chance, I'm opening it right here and now.

TRUFFALDINO. But, it's illegal. Believe me, sir, you don't want a postal worker angry at you.

FLORINDO. This letter is addressed to the one person for whom my opening it would not be a crime. In fact, she would insist upon it. *(Opens letter.)*

TRUFFALDINO. All right sir. It's all yours. *(Muffeletta enters with her exposition sign.)*

FLORINDO. *(Reads.)* "Madam, your departure from this city has given rise to much talk, for all the town now knows that you have gone to join Signor Florindo. The authorities have discovered that you fled dressed as a man and intend to arrest you. I have not sent this letter by the courier from Turin to Venice, because I did not wish to reveal the place to which you have fled, but instead have sent it to a friend at Genoa to be forwarded to Venice. If I have any more news to tell you, I will send it to you by the same semi-circuitous route. Your most humble servant, Antonio." *(Muffeletta exits.)*

TRUFFALDINO. Reading other people's mail. How low can you go.

FLORINDO. *(Aside.)* I am aghast! Beatrice fled to Venice? In man's clothes? To join me? She must love me! If only I can find her. *(Truffaldino knocks on floor.)* Who's there?

TRUFFALDINO. A friend.

FLORINDO. A friend who?

TRUFFALDINO. It's Truffaldino!

FLORINDO. Come in! Truffaldino, find this servant Pasquale, find out who his master is, find out if his master is a man or a woman, find out where he stays, and if you find him first and bring the fellow here you'll get a finder's fee!

TRUFFALDINO. Fair enough. Give me the letter. I'll do what I can.

FLORINDO. There. I'm counting on you. This matter is of the utmost importance to me.

TRUFFALDINO. Should I give him the letter open like this?

FLORINDO. Blame it on a postal worker.

TRUFFALDINO. What about Turin? We still going after dinner?

FLORINDO. Not at the moment. Now off with you and find Pasquale. *(Aside.)* Beatrice in Venice, Federigo in Venice! If Federigo finds her, he'll — No. I will find her first and save her. Beatrice, I'm coming! *(Exits.)*

TRUFFALDINO. I hope I don't lose him. I wanna see how this two master thing works out. After all, it's really a question of balance, a matter of juggling one thing with another, a test of skill and professional expertise. Now! This letter is the one I have to take to my other master — But I can't give him an open letter. I've got to try to fold it *(Tries various awkward folds.)* — and seal it. But how? I saw my grandmother seal a letter with chewed bread once by chewing the bread into a paste and pasting the bread over the seal. I'll try that. *(Takes a piece of bread out of his pocket.)* It's a crime to waste a crust of bread on something like this, but then tampering with the mail is a crime … *(Chews a little bread to seal the letter and accidentally swallows it.)* Oops. I ate it. I'll chew more. *(Same business.)* Oops. Ate it again. Stomach has a mind of its own. Down boy! Ruff! Ruff! One more time. *(Chews again; would like to swallow the bread, but restrains himself and with great difficulty removes the bread from his mouth.)* Success. *(Seals the letter with the bread.)* Oh, that's nice. That's good. I'm very neat. Bingo!

BEATRICE. *(Enters.)* Truffaldino, have you been to the post office?

TRUFFALDINO. Yes, sir.

BEATRICE. Any letters for me?

TRUFFALDINO. One for your sister.

BEATRICE. Good; where is it?

TRUFFALDINO. Here. *(Gives letter.)*

BEATRICE. This letter has been opened and resealed with … bread.

TRUFFALDINO. Bread? Impossible! How'd that happen?!

BEATRICE. *(Dirty look to Truffaldino, opens letter.)* AHA! A letter to me from my servant in Turin informing me that the authorities are after me and that Florindo is in Venice as well. Listen, I have some things to do. Here are my keys. You go to the inn and unpack.

TRUFFALDINO. And we'll eat dinner?

BEATRICE. When I come back. *(Aside.)* No sign of Signor Pantalone, and I need my money. Ah Florindo! *(Exits.)*

TRUFFALDINO. That was good. I mean I knew I was good, but

25

I didn't know I was THAT good. *(Enter Pantalone.)*
PANTALONE. You there! Is your master here?
TRUFFALDINO. No, sir, he isn't.
PANTALONE. Where is he?
TRUFFALDINO. No idea, sir.
PANTALONE. He coming back for lunch?
TRUFFALDINO. I hope so, sir.
PANTALONE. Here. Soon as he comes back, give him this. A hundred ducats. I have to go. Goodbye. *(Exit Pantalone.)*
TRUFFALDINO. G'bye to you too, sir! Funny. He didn't say which master I'm supposed to give it to. *(Enter Florindo.)*
FLORINDO. Truffaldino, did you find Pasquale?
TRUFFALDINO. No, but I did find a gentleman who gave me a hundred ducats.
FLORINDO. A hundred ducats? For what?
TRUFFALDINO. Lemme ask you: were you expecting money from anyone?
FLORINDO. Well ... I had presented a letter of credit to a merchant.
TRUFFALDINO. Then it's yours.
FLORINDO. Great. Now you won't forget Pasquale.
TRUFFALDINO. I'll find him right after dinner.
FLORINDO. Good! Let's go in and get a menu. *(Goes into the inn.)*
TRUFFALDINO. Whoa. That was close. Thank God I gave the money to the right master.

Scene 3

A room in the house of Pantalone.

PANTALONE. You'll marry Signor Federigo, and that's final!
CLARICE. Father, I have always obeyed you, but this is unjust!
PANTALONE. You didn't object the first time you were engaged to him. "Speak then or forever hold your peace"!
CLARICE. My filial duty made me mute.
PANTALONE. Well, duty calls, be mute again! I've made your bed, now lie in it.

CLARICE. My heart is designed for single occupancy! *(Enter Smeraldina.)*

SMERALDINA. Sir, Signor Federigo is here. He wants to speak with you.

CLARICE. *(Weeping.)* This is a nightmare!

SMERALDINA. Come on, Signor Federigo is a fine looking specimen. If I had your luck with men, I wouldn't cry, I'd be dancing in the streets.

PANTALONE. Show him up. *(Exit Smeraldina. To Clarice.)* Enough tears, we don't want him to see you crying.

CLARICE. How can I stop crying when my heart won't stop breaking! *(Enter Beatrice in man's dress.)*

BEATRICE. Signor Pantalone, greetings and salutations.

PANTALONE. Your servant, sir. Did you receive the purse with the hundred ducats?

BEATRICE. No.

PANTALONE. But I just now gave it to your servant. The honest one.

BEATRICE. I must have missed him. Not to worry, I'm sure he'll give me the money when I get back to the inn. *(Clarice weeps, making bleating sounds. Aside to Pantalone.)* What's with the sheep? Is she crying?

PANTALONE. Signor Federigo, when she heard you were dead, she started to cry, and even your miraculous resurrection hasn't stopped the flood.

BEATRICE. Leave us. I'll see if I can stem the tide.

PANTALONE. Certainly, sir. *(To Clarice.)* Sweetheart, Daddy has to run an errand. Entertain your fiancé while I'm gone. Play nice now. *(Exit Pantalone.)*

BEATRICE. Signora Clarice, I —

CLARICE. Don't talk to me! Don't look at me! Don't touch me!

BEATRICE. Getting me used to married life, eh?

CLARICE. Drag me to the altar, you'll hold my fist and nothing more!

BEATRICE. If you knew what we have in common, you wouldn't be afraid.

CLARICE. Pah! Leave me alone!

BEATRICE. But I have the key to quell your qualms.

CLARICE. Only Silvio has my qualm key!

BEATRICE. True, some things only a Silvio can provide. Signora Clarice, do you want to know a secret? You don't want me and I

27

don't want you. Your hand is already taken? Well, so is mine.

CLARICE. Now I'm starting to like you. Wait, is this some trick?

BEATRICE. No trick, madam. And if you promise to keep secret the secret I have just divulged, I will confide in you another secret, designed to deliver unto you some peace of mind.

CLARICE. I vow a vow of silence.

BEATRICE. I am not Federigo Rasponi. I am his sister Beatrice.

CLARICE. *(Shrieks.)* A woman?!

BEATRICE. Why, yes, I am!

CLARICE. But what about your brother? *(Muffeletta enters.)*

BEATRICE. My beloved killed him in a duel, and it is my beloved I am looking for. That's why I'm in disguise. *(Muffeletta exits.)* I beseech you by all the laws of womanly friendship and feminine affection ... do not betray me. I know I shouldn't have told you any of this, but (a) you appeared suicidal, (b) you looked like someone who could keep a secret, and (c) Silvio wants to kill me and I need to defuse him by whatever means necessary. So now that you know the truth ... do you like me better?

CLARICE. Like you? I adore you ... in a sisterly way. From here on, I am your best friend.

BEATRICE. Me too. Give me your hand.

CLARICE. Why, what do you want with it?

BEATRICE. Clarice, if you don't think I'm a woman, I'll show you proof. *(Holds Clarice's hand a bit too close to her breast.)*

CLARICE. It seems unreal.

BEATRICE. No, it's real! Listen, I have to go. Let's take hands in a sign of friendship and loyalty.

CLARICE. Take this my hand. I entrust it to you. *(They embrace. Enter Pantalone.)*

PANTALONE. *(Beams.)* Well, that was quick!

BEATRICE. Signor — !

PANTALONE. Gee, five more minutes I'd be a grandpa! Now we can have the wedding at once!

CLARICE. Oh, but, Father, we mustn't hurry love.

PANTALONE. Now, now, I saw you kissing and hugging. No doubt about it, the wedding's tomorrow.

BEATRICE. Signor Pantalone, don't forget we still have to complete our business and go over our accounts.

PANTALONE. No problem. Take an hour or two at most and then tomorrow the wedding bells ring.

CLARICE. Father, there's still a prob —

PANTALONE. Sweetmeat, I know what you're worried about, but don't be. I'll take care of Silvio.

CLARICE. But you know what Silvio's like when he loses his temper —

PANTALONE. You want two husbands?

CLARICE. Not at the same time, but —

PANTALONE. Then enough with the buts, the problem is solved. G'bye. *(Exit.)*

CLARICE. It's worse now than when you were a man!

BEATRICE. As long as we don't get married, it'll all work out.

CLARICE. But what if Silvio thinks I'm being unfaithful to him?

BEATRICE. Tell him it was a fling.

CLARICE. I want to tell him the truth!

BEATRICE. You made me a vow!

CLARICE. Then what do I do?

BEATRICE. Suffer.

CLARICE. It's not the suffering I mind, it's the *pain* of the suffering.

BEATRICE. If we didn't suffer, we wouldn't be happy. We probably wouldn't even know we're alive.

CLARICE. Fine, I know I'm alive 'cause I'm living in hell!

"Life is suffering
Tempered by hope.
And is it worth it?
I say nope."

Scene 4

The courtyard of Pantalone's house.

SILVIO. Father, please, I have asked you to leave me alone!

DR. LOMBARDI. And I have said I want answers. What are you doing here in Pantalone's courtyard?

SILVIO. Either the man keeps his word to me or he render satisfaction for the affront he has inflicted.

DR. LOMBARDI. Leave him to me, my boy, I know how to talk to him. I'll use reason and logic. I'll make him see the error of his ways. Now, go and wait for me outside. I'll buttonhole Signor

Pantalone.

SILVIO. But Father —

DR. LOMBARDI. Silvio! Do I have to count to three?

SILVIO. No, sir. I'll go, sir. I'll wait for you at the apothecary's. But if Signor Pantalone won't listen to reason, tell him he'll have me to deal with! *(Exit Silvio.)*

DR. LOMBARDI. Poor kid, can't help but pity him. Pantalone should never have agreed to him marrying Clarice unless he knew for certain that fellow from Turin was dead. I'll discuss the issue with him, reasonably, with decorum. I just hope I don't lose my famous temper. *(Enter Pantalone.)*

PANTALONE. *(Aside.)* What's the doctor doing here?

DR. LOMBARDI. Your servant, Signor Pantalone.

PANTALONE. Your servant, Doctor Lombardi. I was just coming to look for you and your son.

DR. LOMBARDI. You were? Oh, what a relief! Signora Clarice is to be Silvio's wife, after all?

PANTALONE. *(Much embarrassed.)* Well, actually —

DR. LOMBARDI. No need for explanations. It was an awkward situation. Let's let bygones be bygones.

PANTALONE. Yes, well, about that promise I made Signor Federigo —

DR. LOMBARDI. He blindsided you! Took you by surprise, no time to think! I'm sure you never even realized how much you were going to insult and offend my entire family.

PANTALONE. Well … insults and offenses notwithstanding, there had been a previous contract —

DR. LOMBARDI. Oh, you don't have to tell me. A contract is a binding agreement, forged in honor and locked in law. But that was a two-way contract between you and the fellow from Turin, whereas ours is a threesome, confirmed in its validity by the love of the girl herself.

PANTALONE. Yes, but —

DR. LOMBARDI. And as you know, in matrimonial cases, *consensus, et non concubitus, facit virum.*

PANTALONE. My Latin is a little rusty —

DR. LOMBARDI. "Women cannot be sacrificed."

PANTALONE. … Any other pearls of wisdom?

DR. LOMBARDI. Nothing else.

PANTALONE. So you're finished?

DR. LOMBARDI. I'm finished.

PANTALONE. May I speak?

DR. LOMBARDI. You may.

PANTALONE. Doctor, you may have the advantage of a higher education, but —

DR. LOMBARDI. Of course there's the question of the dowry, but that's negotiable, by and large, give or take.

PANTALONE. … Lemme start again. May I speak?

DR. LOMBARDI. Speak!

PANTALONE. Then LISTEN: I have great respect for legal learning, but in this case it does not apply.

DR. LOMBARDI. Are you trying to tell me the OTHER marriage is still going to take place?

PANTALONE. I gave my word, I can't back out! And now that my daughter has fallen in love with Signor Rasponi, there are no more stumbling blocks.

DR. LOMBARDI. "Fallen in…?!" You appall me, sir! There will be penalties to pay, sir, compensation, pain and suffering and court costs! Gentlemen of the jury, a marriage contract contracted prior to the dissolution of a prior contract cannot be dissolved by contracting a further contract unless the prior contract has been contracted prior to the dissolution of the former. *Coram testibus, omna tempus, tempus fugat, ute lemper, bupkes! (Exit Doctor.)*

PANTALONE. Yeah, well, go to hell, ya Latin gasbag! The Rasponis can buy and sell the Lombardis, *E PLURIBUS UNUM! (Enter Silvio.)*

SILVIO. *(Aside.)* — Hold my temper? My temper will not be bridled, for temper is as temper does!

PANTALONE. Gasbag, the Younger.

SILVIO. My father has just related to me news which I can scarce believe is true. The marriage contract between Signora Clarice and Signor Federigo is settled?

PANTALONE. Settled, finished, over, done.

SILVIO. OH! How can you even show your face! You have no honor, no sense of what it means to be a gentleman — !

PANTALONE. Excuse me? Is this how a "gentleman" talks to a man of my age — ?

SILVIO. So you're old! You'll be easier to stab!

PANTALONE. I am not a shish-kabob, sir, to be skewered and turned on a spit! What right do you have to come into my home and make threats?

SILVIO. You have a point. Let's go outside.

PANTALONE. I am a gentleman, accustomed to being treated with respect.

SILVIO. You are a weasel, accustomed to being a weasel!

PANTALONE. You dog! You boy! You dog-boy!

SILVIO. By heavens, I shall strike thee — ! *(Lays his hand to his sword.)*

PANTALONE. Help! Murder! *(Beatrice enters and draws her sword.)*

BEATRICE. Father-in-law, I shall defend you!

PANTALONE. Son-in-law! Just in time!

SILVIO. Ah-ha, the very man my sword has sought!

BEATRICE. *(Aside.)* Not who I wanted to bump into.

PANTALONE. He'll put so many holes in you, they'll call you Sieve-io.

SILVIO. Come, sir, steel to steel?

PANTALONE. Son-in-law, save me!

BEATRICE. Never fear, Father, I've fought far finer foes!

PANTALONE. Help! Help! *(Pantalone runs off. Beatrice and Silvio fight. Silvio falls and drops his sword. Beatrice holds her point to his heart. Enter Clarice.)*

CLARICE. *(To Beatrice.)* No, stop!

BEATRICE. Sweetest Clarice. Because you so tenderly utter your request I will with much regret tender to Silvio his life, and in consideration of my mercy, I but beg you to remember your solemn VOW. *(Exit Beatrice.)*

CLARICE. Dearest Silvio, are you hurt?

SILVIO. "Dearest Silvio!" Dear to her who mocks and cuckolds him!

CLARICE. Silvio, why such reproach? I love you, I adore you, I am faithful to you!

SILVIO. Infidelity, thy name is Clarice! Faithful, yes, but to me, HA! You call faithful your VOW to wed another?

CLARICE. I never vowed to wed another. I'd die before I'd lose you.

SILVIO. But he just said "remember your solemn VOW."

CLARICE. But that is not a vow of matrimony.

SILVIO. Then what kind of vow is it?

CLARICE. Dear Silvio, I wish I could explain the vow, but I can't.

SILVIO. Why not?

CLARICE. Because I made a vow.

SILVIO. To whom have you made this vow?

CLARICE. Federigo.

SILVIO. And I believed you when you said you loved me! Only a fool rides a horse called "Woman"!

CLARICE. I love you with all my heart.

SILVIO. I hate you with all my ... spleen.

CLARICE. Silvio, I will kill myself if you don't stop this!

SILVIO. Better dead, than Federigo's.

CLARICE. Fine, then, I hope you'll be satisfied! *(Picks up his sword.)*

SILVIO. Yeah, that'll do.

CLARICE. You're being very cruel to me!

SILVIO. 'Twas from your lips I learned the way.

CLARICE. Then you want me to die? *(Points the sword at her breast. Enter Smeraldina.)*

SMERALDINA. Whoa-ho! What's going on? *(Takes the sword away from Clarice. To Silvio.)* What were you gonna do, let her stab herself while you sit on your buns? *(To Clarice.)* Don't tell me: he decided he doesn't want you anymore. Little saying: The man who does not WANT you is the man who does not DESERVE you. *(To Silvio.)* Girl-killer! Tell him to bug off and get on with your life. *(She throws down the sword; Silvio picks it up.)*

CLARICE. Ingrate! That I should — that I should — *(Forgets her line; calls to Prompter.)* LINE! *(The Prompter smiles up at Clarice.)* LINE! *(Prompter gives a note to Smeraldina. Smeraldina reads the note.)*

SMERALDINA. He's mute.

CLARICE. What?

SMERALDINA. HE'S MUTE! THE PROMPTER'S MUTE!

CLARICE. Can't you give me the lines?

SMERALDINA. *(Shakes head.)* Union rules. *(Clarice fumes and turns back to the Prompter.)*

CLARICE. Ingrate! That I should — *(Prompter hits his chest.)* — hit myself in the chest. *(Prompter closes his eyes.)* That I should take a nap. *(Prompter folds hands over chest. Clarice gets it.)* "That I should DIE — !" *(Clarice turns to Silvio.)* "That I should die and you not heave a single sigh! Well, I shall die and die of GRIEF, and when I do, you'll get your wish and know that I was — " *(Prompter holds up finger.)*

SMERALDINA. One word. *(Prompter taps arm three times.)*

SILVIO. Three syllables. *(Prompter mimes rocking a baby.)*

CLARICE. A baby. *(Prompter bats his eyes.)* Blinking. *(Prompter makes a face.)* Stupid. You'll know I was a stupid, blinking baby. *(Prompter starts making crazy signals.)*

SILVIO. Steal home! Stay on third! Be ready to bunt! *(Prompter points to Silvio.)*

SMERALDINA. Nitwit ... INNOCENT! *(Prompter points at Smeraldina and claps.)*
SILVIO. *(Jumps up and down.)* DING! DING! DING! DING! DING!
CLARICE. YOU'LL KNOW THAT I WAS INNOCENT, AND IT'LL BE TOO LATE, AND YOU'LL BE THE ONE CRYING THEN! *(Clarice, Silvio and Smeraldina cheer and jump. Prompter collapses, exhausted.)* I am never going to tour again! *(Clarice strides off.)*
SMERALDINA. I don't get it: You got a girl with a sword on the point of killing herself, and you sit there like you're watching a play.
SILVIO. Oh, come on! The sword she held was nowhere near her heart.
SMERALDINA. It was in the general vicinity.
SILVIO. You're a woman ...
SMERALDINA. AND?
SILVIO. Women have imaginations.
SMERALDINA. And what women do, men can't imagine. *(Smeraldina sings and exits.)*

Scene 5

A room in Brighella's inn, with a door at each side and two doors at the back, facing the audience.

TRUFFALDINO. Well, I'm mortified! Two masters and not a one back for lunch. Two o'clock, and zip for duo! You know what's gonna happen: they're both gonna show up at the same time, and I'll be the one caught in the middle. I won't be able to juggle 'em both, and the jig will be up. Wait! Shh! Here comes one of 'em. A bird in the hand is worth two birds not handy. *(Enter Florindo.)*
FLORINDO. Truffaldino, did you find your friend Pasquale?
TRUFFALDINO. I thought I was supposed to look for him after lunch.
FLORINDO. I'd like to find him sooner rather than later.
TRUFFALDINO. Then we should've had lunch sooner.
FLORINDO. *(Aside.)* How am I going to find out if Beatrice is

here?

TRUFFALDINO. *(Aside.)* First he tells me to order lunch, then he goes off gallivanting who knows where while lunch comes and lunch goes —

FLORINDO. I don't want to eat! *(Aside.)* The post office! Maybe I can find out something there myself.

TRUFFALDINO. Not eat? But, sir, you know the saying: "When in Venice, eat, or you'll fall off your feet."

FLORINDO. Have to go; important business. If I come back, I'll eat, if not, I'll grab a bite later. You want lunch, order it yourself.

TRUFFALDINO. Oh, yes, sir, very good, sir, as you wish, sir; you're the master.

FLORINDO. Oh, and here, take this money and put it in my trunk. Don't forget the key. *(Gives Truffaldino the purse and his keys.)*

TRUFFALDINO. Right here sir. *(Indicating pouch.)*

FLORINDO. If I'm not back by lunch, come to the plaza. I will not rest until we've found this Pasquale. *(Exit Florindo. Muffeletta enters.)*

TRUFFALDINO. Okay, what was the main point to remember from that scene? That he said I could go ahead and eat. *Muffeletta exits.)* We're all agreed on that, right? I mean, if he doesn't want to eat, fine, but my complexion is not made for fasting. I'll just stash his purse, and then I'll go. *(Enter Beatrice.)*

BEATRICE. Truffaldino!

TRUFFALDINO. *(Aside.)* Drat! My day job!

BEATRICE. Did Signor Pantalone dei Bisognosi give you a purse with a hundred ducats?

TRUFFALDINO. Yes, indeed he did.

BEATRICE. Why didn't you give it to me?

TRUFFALDINO. Was it yours?

BEATRICE. Was it mine? What did he say when he gave it to you?

TRUFFALDINO. He said to give it to my master.

BEATRICE. And who is your master?

TRUFFALDINO. You are.

BEATRICE. Then why did you ask if the money was mine?

TRUFFALDINO. … Double checking.

BEATRICE. So where is it?

TRUFFALDINO. Right here, sir. *(Gives Beatrice the purse.)*

BEATRICE. *(Aside.)* I'll count it later. Is the innkeeper around?

TRUFFALDINO. Yes, sir.

BEATRICE. Tell him I'm having a guest for lunch. Table for two.

Pronto!

TRUFFALDINO. Yes, sir, may I take your order? Will you have something to start?

BEATRICE. Signor Pantalone won't expect much. Five or six dishes; take your pick.

TRUFFALDINO. You're leaving it to me?

BEATRICE. Use your judgment, for whatever that's worth. He's not far, so make sure it's ready by the time we get back. *(Going.)*

TRUFFALDINO. On the double, sir!

BEATRICE. Oh, and put this in my trunk. Don't lose it, it's a bank check for four thousand ducats.

TRUFFALDINO. Trust me, sir, I'll hide it at once.

BEATRICE. Do that! *(Exit Beatrice.)*

TRUFFALDINO. This is my moment. My destiny calls me: This is the first time this master has ordered me to order dinner. I'll show him I'm a man of taste. I'll just put away this check and then — no, later, mustn't waste time. Hey in there! Anybody home? *(Calling into the inn.)* Brighella? *(Returning.)* The key to a really memorable meal is not a mountain of food in the middle of the table, but a beautifully laid setting. *(Enter Brighella.)*

BRIGHELLA. What is it, Signor Truffaldino? What can I do for you?

TRUFFALDINO. My master has a gentleman coming to lunch. He wants something good and quick. Kitchen stocked?

BRIGHELLA. Half an hour, I whip up whatever you want.

TRUFFALDINO. All right then, what comes with what?

BRIGHELLA. First course, we got soup, fried fish, boiled meat, and a fricandeau.

TRUFFALDINO. I know the first three, but tell me Brighella, what's a fricandeau?

BRIGHELLA. Kind of a ragout. It's French for ... "tastes good."

TRUFFALDINO. Good, that's the first course. What's the second?

BRIGHELLA. Second course: duck, salad, meat pie — and trifle.

TRUFFALDINO. *(Indignant.)* A trifle? These men are big men, hungry men, they won't be satisfied with a trifle!

BRIGHELLA. Trifle is a dessert, a pudding, it's from England.

TRUFFALDINO. *(Nonchalantly.)* Oh. Well. If it's "English," I'm sure it'll be ... flavorful. We'll have that. All right, how about setting the table.

BRIGHELLA. Don't worry about the table, the waiter'll take care of the table.

TRUFFALDINO. Uh … excuse me, friend, but laying a table is not something that can be "delegated." This is my master's table. *(Does bit with check, using it to describe the table and in the process, tears it into little pieces.)*
BRIGHELLA. No, the master's table is there.
TRUFFALDINO. No, this is my master's table.
BRIGHELLA. No, the table is there.
TRUFFALDINO. Well, just imagine for a second that this is my master's table.
BRIGHELLA. Okay. *(Truffaldino and Brighella continue to improvise the placement of table and then continue with:)*
TRUFFALDINO. Here are five dishes and in the middle the soup. *(He tears off a piece of the check and puts it on the floor to represent a dish.)* Now the boiled meat. *(Same business.)* … put the fried here, *(Same business.)* here the gravy and here that — tasty frickin' French stuff. See? A well-laid table! It's a good thing!
BRIGHELLA. Uh-huh … you got your gravy a mile away from your meat.
TRUFFALDINO. All right, so we move it closer. *(Improvise placement of dishes using ripped check. Enter Beatrice and Pantalone.)*
BEATRICE. What are you two doing?
TRUFFALDINO. *(Stands up.)* I was just arranging the table setting.
BEATRICE. What's that paper?
TRUFFALDINO. *(Aside.)* YIPES! The check he gave me!
BEATRICE. Is that my check?
TRUFFALDINO. I'm very sorry, sir; lemme put it right back together again.
BEATRICE. You lowlife! Is this how you take care of my things? You should be beaten repeatedly!
TRUFFALDINO. I'll do it myself. *(Improvise beating.)*
BEATRICE. Signor Pantalone? Have you ever seen anything like this?
PANTALONE. Tell you the truth, I was too busy laughing. Ahem, of course, it would be serious if it couldn't be fixed but I'll write you another check, it'll be fine.
BEATRICE. Thank you. *(To Truffaldino.)* You're an idiot!
TRUFFALDINO. It's all because Brighella doesn't know how to lay a table.
BRIGHELLA. Everything's my fault!
TRUFFALDINO. Some men know how to lay a table —
BEATRICE. *(To Truffaldino.)* Get out of here.

TRUFFALDINO. Got to lay tables the right way …

BEATRICE. Go, get out, now! *(Truffaldino exits.)*

BRIGHELLA. I don't get that guy. He's like an enigma wrapped inside a conundrum wrapped inside an idiot. Anything particular you fancy for lunch?

PANTALONE. Two meatballs. For the sake of my two teeth.

BEATRICE. You hear? Meatballs.

BRIGHELLA. Very good, sir. Sit down, please, gentlemen, lunch will be up shortly.

BEATRICE. And tell Truffaldino to come wait on us.

BRIGHELLA. I'll tell him, sir. *(Exit Brighella.)*

BEATRICE. Just our luck: potluck.

PANTALONE. Oh, sir, I accept your kind hospitality. Frankly, it cheers me up. I'm still a little shaky from this morning. If you hadn't saved me from that young scoundrel Silvio, he would've run me through.

BEATRICE. I'm just glad I got there in time. *(Waiters enter from the kitchen and carry glasses, wine, bread, etc., into the room where Beatrice and Pantalone are to dine.)*

PANTALONE. Quick service. *(Enter Truffaldino carrying the soup tureen.)*

TRUFFALDINO. *(To Beatrice.)* Lunch is served, sir. This way please.

BEATRICE. Go and put the soup on the table.

TRUFFALDINO. *(Makes a bow.)* After you, sir.

PANTALONE. You have a very strange servant. *(Goes in.)*

BEATRICE. *(To Truffaldino.)* Personally, I would prefer less servant and more service. *(Goes in.)*

TRUFFALDINO. And they call that dinner! One dish at a time! These guys got money to burn, but nothing to show for it. I doubt this soup is even worth eating; I better check it. *(Takes a spoon out of his pocket and tastes the soup.)* Thank goodness I'm always armed. Not bad; could be worse. *(Goes into room with soup. Enter First Waiter with a dish.)*

FIRST WAITER. When is that guy coming to take this dish?

TRUFFALDINO. *(Reentering.)* Here, friend. What you got for me?

FIRST WAITER. Boiled meat. Another dish to follow. *(Exit First Waiter.)*

TRUFFALDINO. What is this? Mutton? Or veal? Mutton, I think. I better check it. *(Tastes.)* Nope, not mutton, not veal. Lamb. And not lame lamb at that. *(Goes toward Beatrice's room.*

Enter Florindo.)
FLORINDO. Where are you going?
TRUFFALDINO. *(Aside.)* Uh-uh-oh!
FLORINDO. What are you doing with that dish?
TRUFFALDINO. I was just putting it on the table, sir.
FLORINDO. For whom?
TRUFFALDINO. For youm.
FLORINDO. Why are you serving my dinner before I've arrived?
TRUFFALDINO. I saw you coming from an upstairs windowl
FLORINDO. So you start with boiled meat and then have soup after?
TRUFFALDINO. In Venice, sir, the soup is always supped last.
FLORINDO. Yes, well, not being from Venice, I'd like my soup first. Take that boiled thing back to the kitchen.
TRUFFALDINO. Yes, sir, as you wish, sir.
FLORINDO. And hurry, I want to eat, then take a nap.
TRUFFALDINO. Yes, sir. *(Makes as if going to the kitchen.)*
FLORINDO. *(Aside.)* Ah, Beatrice. *(Florindo goes into the other room. As soon as he is in, Truffaldino quickly takes the dish in to Beatrice. Enter First Waiter with another dish. Florindo calls from his room.)*
FIRST WAITER. How long am I supposed to wait? Truffaldino!
TRUFFALDINO. *(Coming out of Beatrice's room.)* Coming, sir. *(To First Waiter.)* Quick, set a table in that room, the other gentleman has arrived — and bring the soup!
FIRST WAITER. Right! *(Exit First Waiter.)*
TRUFFALDINO. What's this stuff? Ah, must be the "fricandeau." Better check it. *(Tastes it.)* Say, that's French for "tastes good." *(Takes it in to Beatrice. Waiters enter and carry glasses, wine, bread, etc., into Florindo's room. To Waiters.)* Good, right, go, bravo! *(Aside.)* Wait on two tables for two masters, I'm too much! *(The Waiters come back out of Florindo's room and go toward the kitchen.)* All right, soup's on, let's go, go, go!
FIRST WAITER. Hey, wait on your own table, we got this one. *(Exeunt Waiters.)*
TRUFFALDINO. No, I'm pumped, I wanna play doubles! *(Reenter First Waiter with Florindo's soup.)* Gimme that, you get the stuff for the other room. *(Takes soup from First Waiter and carries it into Florindo's room.)*
FIRST WAITER. Let him wait on the whole restaurant; we split the tips anyway. *(Truffaldino comes out of Florindo's room.)*
BEATRICE. *(Calling from her room.)* Truffaldino!

FIRST WAITER. *(To Truffaldino.)* Your master's calling.

TRUFFALDINO. Coming sir. *(Goes into Beatrice's room. Second Waiter brings the boiled meat for Florindo. Truffaldino brings the dirty plates out of Beatrice's room. Exit Second Waiter.)*

FLORINDO. *(Calls.)* Truffaldino!

TRUFFALDINO. *(Wishes to take the meat from Waiter.)* Give it to me.

FIRST WAITER. No, I got that!

TRUFFALDINO. Didn't you hear him call for me? *(Takes meat from him and carries it in to Florindo.)*

FIRST WAITER. Fine, it ain't my station. *(Second Waiter brings in a dish of meatballs, gives it to the First Waiter and exits. Reenter Truffaldino from Florindo's room with dirty plates.)* Hey, Super Waiter! Take these meatballs to your master.

TRUFFALDINO. *(Takes dish.)* Meatballs?

FIRST WAITER. He ordered meatballs. *(Exit First Waiter.)*

TRUFFALDINO. He did, huh? Which "he"? If I ask in the kitchen, they'll begin to suspect; if I serve 'em to the wrong one, the other will ask and my cover will be blown. I know; I'll divide the meatballs on two plates, take half to each, and see who claims 'em. *(Takes plates and divides the meatballs.)* That's four and four. And one left over. Who should get the extra? Mustn't cause ill-feeling; I'll force it down myself. *(Eats it.)* Now. We'll take these meatballs to this gentleman. *(Truffaldino puts one plate of meatballs on the floor and takes the other in to Beatrice. First Waiter enters with an English pudding.)*

FIRST WAITER. Truffaldino!

TRUFFALDINO. *(Comes out of Beatrice's room.)* Coming!

FLORINDO. Truffaldino!

TRUFFALDINO. Going!

FIRST WAITER. Truffaldino, take this English pudding to your master. *(Takes the other dish of meatballs and is going to Florindo's room.)*

TRUFFALDINO. *(Reentering.)* What is this sludge?

FIRST WAITER. English pudding.

TRUFFALDINO. And it's for?

FIRST WAITER. Your master. *(Exit First Waiter.)*

TRUFFALDINO. "English pudding"? Smells sweet, looks like green polenta. Better check it. *(Brings a spoon out of his pocket and tries the pudding.)* Like polenta, but not polenta. *(Goes on eating.)* Much better than polenta!

BEATRICE. *(Calling.)* Truffaldino!

TRUFFALDINO. *(With mouth full.)* Coming, sir.

40

FLORINDO. *(Calling.)* Truffaldino!
TRUFFALDINO. *(With mouth full.)* Coming, sir. *(To himself.)*
Oh, this is good stuff! Just one more mouthful and then I'll go.
(Goes on eating.)
BEATRICE/FLORINDO. Truffaldino! *(Truffaldino goes into
kitchen with pudding, then reappears with trays used to shield each
master from the other.)*
BEATRICE. *(Comes out of her room.)* Where is he? Truffaldino! *(Goes
into kitchen.)*
FLORINDO. *(Comes out of his room.)* Where in blazes is he?
Truffaldino! *(Goes into kitchen.)*
BEATRICE. *(Comes out of kitchen.)* Truffaldino! *(Goes into kitchen.)*
FLORINDO. *(Comes out of kitchen.)* Truffaldino! *(Goes into kitchen.)*
BEATRICE. *(Comes out of kitchen.)* Truffaldino! *(Goes into kitchen.)*
FLORINDO. *(Comes out of kitchen.)* Truffaldino! *(Goes into kitchen.)*
TRUFFALDINO. Yes, sir?
BEATRICE. *(Comes out of kitchen, sees Truffaldino.)* There you are.
TRUFFALDINO. Yes, sir?
FLORINDO. *(Comes out of kitchen, sees Truffaldino.)* There you are.
BEATRICE. Come in here and wait on me. *(She goes back to her
room.)*
FLORINDO. Come in here and wait on me. *(Starts toward his
room, as Truffaldino exits to kitchen with trays, then reappears with
pudding. Florindo turns back.)* What are you doing out here? I've
been waiting!
TRUFFALDINO. I went to get the next course, sir.
FLORINDO. Is there anything more to eat?
TRUFFALDINO. I'll go and see.
FLORINDO. Well, hurry, I told you I wanted to take a nap as
soon as I've eaten. *(Goes back into his room.)*
TRUFFALDINO. Very good, sir. *(Calling.)* Waiter, is there any-
thing left in there? *(Aside.)* Save the pudding for later. *(Hides it.
Enter First Waiter with dish.)*
FIRST WAITER. Duck up!
TRUFFALDINO. *(Takes the duck.)* Bring on dessert!
FIRST WAITER. It's coming, it's coming! *(Exit First Waiter.)*
FLORINDO. Take it away.
FIRST WAITER. Fruit up.
BEATRICE. All done.
SECOND WAITER. Fruit up!
FLORINDO. Take this back.

TRUFFALDINO. Didn't like the meatballs.
FIRST WAITER. Dessert up!
SECOND WAITER. Cookies up! Tart up!
FIRST WAITER. Struedel!
FLORINDO. Truffaldino!
FIRST WAITER. Cake up.
SECOND WAITER. Cream up!
FIRST WAITER. Check up!
TRUFFALDINO. *(Reentering.)* All done! They're full! Nobody wants anymore. It's finished!
FLORINDO. Truffaldino!
TRUFFALDINO. The dishes!
BEATRICE. Truffaldino! *(All the Waiters toss plates back and forth with Truffaldino. Truffaldino juggles them with great aplomb, never dropping one. At the end, he turns to the audience. He holds a plate stacked high with food ...)*
TRUFFALDINO. Let's eat!

End of Act One

ACT TWO

Prologue

The Young Woman enters again calling.

YOUNG WOMAN. Mario! Mario! Mario! *(A Stage Hand enters eating a leg of what looks like chicken and then coughs up a feather. Young Woman sees this and wails ...)* MARIO! *(Young Woman chases the Stage Hand offstage. The actors playing Pantalone and Beatrice enter arguing.)*

PANTALONE. ... Don't want to hear another word!

BEATRICE. When I was hired, I was told I could wear a beautiful gown in the last scene! *(Clarice enters.)*

PANTALONE. The script says you wear "manly masculine garb" and you will remain dressed in manly masculine garb right through the curtain call! You want a beautiful gown, write your own play! *(Smeraldina enters with Silvio.)* Where is he?

SMERALDINA. He's backstage. Coughing into his handkerchief.

PANTALONE. Again?

SILVIO. After the plate scene I saw him shaking, wrapped in a blanket.

SMERALDINA. If he doesn't get better, we'll have to stop the show!

PANTALONE. He wants to go on.

SMERALDINA. And so?

PANTALONE. And so he'll go on.

SILVIO. But all the things he has to do in the second act —

PANTALONE. He'll do them, like he does every night. And he'll be good!

SMERALDINA. Yeah, well, you're only as good as your last performance. Sorry. I didn't mean that the way it sounded. *(Smeraldina and Silvio exit.)*

PANTALONE. Ladies and gentlemen, we'll return to this evening's performance in just a moment, but before we do: The fol-

lowing is a paid advertisement. *(Exits. Stage Manager enters, holds his stomach and does some bad acting.)*
STAGE MANAGER. Oh. Oh. Oh. I wish I hadn't eaten those speecy, spicey meatballs. How can I spell relief? *(Patron enters.)*
PATRON. F. R. I. C. A. N. D. E. A. U. What's Fricandeau? I'm glad you asked. Fricandeau is not just ANY patent elixir. No. Fricandeau is a natural medicinal tonic deprived from plants, herbs, fibrous roots and sandworms, used for ages by the ancient tribes of the Guappawooshkee on the Isle of Kikoman. Is Fricandeau a purgatory? Oh, yes. Is it a binding agent? You bet! Does it make the blind walk and the lame see? Yes, yes, and oh, yes … YES. But don't believe me, believe the testimony of someone who's tried Fricandeau. Oh, stage manager? The stage manager recently suffered from those age-old seasonal maladies known as posterior bunions, nasal wart clusters, and Satanic possession.
STAGE MANAGER. I was ready to throw up … my hands. *(Gestures.)*
PATRON. Then he tried —
STAGE MANAGER. "Fricandeau."
PATRON. And now?
STAGE MANAGER. I got rid of the warts and bunions, and my satanic possession is under control. Thanks, Fricandeau! *(Exits.)*
PATRON. And thank you, Stage Manager. Y'know, the stage manager is just one of thousands upon thousands of satisfied Fricandeau users. And now please welcome Smeraldina and the Fricandelles. *(Singers enter.)*
SINGERS.
> When you're sick,
> And you need something quick,
> Oh,
> Something quick
> And it's got to have quite a kick.
> Try Fricandeau.
> It's fast, not slow.
> Put down the dough,
> You'll go, go, go!
> Just pretend it's Mexico,
> When you go
> With Fricandeau.
> Side effects
> May include loss of sex

Drive
Loss of sex
Drive;
It'll take a nosedive.
It's *comme-il-faut*
With Fricandeau.
It's come and go,
Win, place, or show.
Say goodbye to Romeo
When you go
With Fricandeau.
Please, please buy some Fricandeau.
STAGE MANAGER. Places! ACT TWO! *(They all exit. Act Two begins.)*

Scene 1

A street outside Brighella's inn. Enter Smeraldina.

SMERALDINA. Well! All I can say is that my young lady is NO LADY! My mistress sends me all alone through the streets with a message to this emporium of sin and spirits! It's hard to be a lady-in-waiting who waits on a lady in love! If she loves Silvio so much that she's willing to disembowel herself for him, why is she sending messages to this other fellow? That girl goes through men like a Kraut through bratwurst. This is the tavern, and here I am, but I won't go inside. I'll make 'em come out. Hello! Anybody home? If my master sees me, what will I say? I know! I'll tell him I came to look for him. See, I'm smart when pressed. Hey in there! *(Enter Truffaldino with a bottle in his hand, a glass and a napkin.)*
TRUFFALDINO. Yeah, who sent for me? And keep your hands off my Fricandeau. *(Patron darts on, tosses Truffaldino a coin, and darts off.)*
SMERALDINA. Me, sir. I hope I haven't disturbed you.
TRUFFALDINO. Nooooo! Your pleasure is my duty.
SMERALDINA. I don't want to interrupt your lunch.
TRUFFALDINO. Don't worry, you won't. I was full to bursting,

but your effervescent eyes are just what I need to help me digest.

SMERALDINA. *(Aside.)* OH! A poet! *(Truffaldino burps.)*

TRUFFALDINO. I'll just put down this bottle, and then I'll lend an ear, dear.

SMERALDINA. *(Aside.)* And he rhymes! *(To Truffaldino.)* My mistress sent this letter to Signor Federigo Rasponi. I didn't want to come inside the tavern, so I thought I might ask you to deliver it, seeing as you're his man.

TRUFFALDINO. With pleasure; but first, I have a message for you.

SMERALDINA. From who?

TRUFFALDINO. From a good man, an honest man, an upstanding man. Tell me, are you acquainted with one Truffaldino Battocchio?

SMERALDINA. I've heard a word or two, but nothing solid.

TRUFFALDINO. He's handsome, stocky, swarthy, smart, and a heck of a maître d'.

SMERALDINA. Don't know him.

TRUFFALDINO. He knows you. He loves you.

SMERALDINA. Stop! You're teasing me!

TRUFFALDINO. And if he can glimpse a small sign of affection he would make himself known.

SMERALDINA. Well, maybe if I met him and liked him I could return his affection.

TRUFFALDINO. Wanna see him?

SMERALDINA. Please.

TRUFFALDINO. Be right back. *(Goes into the inn. Truffaldino comes out of the inn, makes low bows to Smeraldina, passes close to her, sighs, and goes back into the inn.)*

SMERALDINA. Did I miss something?

TRUFFALDINO. *(Reentering.)* Did you see him?

SMERALDINA. Who?

TRUFFALDINO. That man in love with your titillating beauty.

SMERALDINA. All I saw was you.

TRUFFALDINO. *(Sighs.)* Uh-huh.

SMERALDINA. So you're the mystery lover?

TRUFFALDINO. Oh, yeaaaah. *(Sighs.)*

SMERALDINA. Why didn't you say so before?

TRUFFALDINO. Just shy, I guess.

SMERALDINA. *(Aside.)* The man could seduce a slab a' beef!

TRUFFALDINO. Well, what do you say?

SMERALDINA. I dunno —

TRUFFALDINO. What do you say?
SMERALDINA. I dunno —
TRUFFALDINO. What do you say?
SMERALDINA. I dunno —
TRUFFALDINO. Say something!
SMERALDINA. *(Grabs him.)* I'M SHY TOO!
TRUFFALDINO. Great! If we got married we'd be two married shy people. But wait a minute, have you ever been a bride before?
SMERALDINA. What a question!
TRUFFALDINO. That means "yes"?
SMERALDINA. That means "no." I could've had dozens of husbands, but I never found the right one.
TRUFFALDINO. Well, then — is there any hope for me?
SMERALDINA. Well — to tell the truth — there is something about you — Enough, I won't say it.
TRUFFALDINO. Look, if somebody wanted to marry you, who would he have to ask?
SMERALDINA. My master and mistress.
TRUFFALDINO. Say I ask. What do they say?
SMERALDINA. They'll say they're happy if I'm happy.
TRUFFALDINO. And what'll you say?
SMERALDINA. I'll say I'm happy if they're happy.
TRUFFALDINO. Good, then, we're all going to be happy. Give me the letter and when I bring back the answer, we'll talk.
SMERALDINA. Here's the letter.
TRUFFALDINO. You don't happen to know what's in it?
SMERALDINA. No, but I'm dying to find out!
TRUFFALDINO. Well, if I don't know what's in it, I can't carry it inside. It's a matter of ethics.
SMERALDINA. We could open it — but how do we seal it again?
TRUFFALDINO. Honey, "sealing letters" is my middle name.
SMERALDINA. Then open it!
TRUFFALDINO. Let's do this neatly. *(Opens it.)* There. It's open.
SMERALDINA. Quick, read it.
TRUFFALDINO. The letter says ...
SMERALDINA. The letter says ...
TRUFFALDINO. The letter says ...
SMERALDINA. The letter says ...
TRUFFALDINO. The letter says ... there isn't enough light. You read it. You're more closely acquainted with your mistress' handwriting.

SMERALDINA. *(Looking at the letter.)* She has lousy handwriting. I can't make out a word.

TRUFFALDINO. Wait, let me see it again. I know, let's BOTH work on the letters one by one, like a team.

SMERALDINA. Well, the first word is "Dear."

TRUFFALDINO. "Dear." How do you know it's "Dear"?

SMERALDINA. Because it's a letter.

TRUFFALDINO. Oh. Clever. Well, I think this letter after "Dear" is an S. *(Letter improv.)*

SMERALDINA. Well, if that's an S, then the next letter is an I.

TRUFFALDINO. How do you know?

SMERALDINA. *(Cuddling into his lap.)* See it's kind of long and hard and it has a big bulging head on it.

TRUFFALDINO. *(Excited.)* WHOA! Well then, if it's an S and an I, the word must be "Sir." "Dear Sir"!

SMERALDINA. No, it's not "Sir," see? The letter after I is another S. *(Letter improv.)*

BOTH. S I S, S I S, S I S … SISTER! "Dear Sister"!

TRUFFALDINO. That doesn't make sense. He's her fiancé. He's my master. Why would your mistress call my mister "Sister"?

SMERALDINA. The upper classes are well known for their in-breeding. *(Beatrice comes out of the inn with Pantalone.)*

PANTALONE. Smeraldina, what are you doing here?

SMERALDINA. Sir! I was just coming to look for you.

BEATRICE. Say, what's this?

TRUFFALDINO. *(Frightened.)* Nothing, piece a' paper —

BEATRICE. Let me see.

TRUFFALDINO. *(Gives paper, trembling.)* Yes, sir.

BEATRICE. Another letter addressed to me, and you opened it! Do you do this for a living?

TRUFFALDINO. I am completely in the dark about this.

BEATRICE. Signor Pantalone, I received a letter from Signora Clarice informing me of Silvio's insane jealousy, and this villain has the impudence to tear it open!

PANTALONE. *(To Smeraldina.)* And you helped him?

SMERALDINA. I'm in the dark too, sir.

BEATRICE. Then who opened the letter?

SMERALDINA. Not I.

TRUFFALDINO. Not I either.

PANTALONE. Well, who brought it?

SMERALDINA. Truffaldino brought it to his master.

TRUFFALDINO. And Smeraldina brought it to Truffaldino.

SMERALDINA. Squealer! I don't love you anymore!

TRUFFALDINO. I don't love you either, squealer!

PANTALONE. So, young lady, you're the cause of all this trouble! I've a good mind to give you a thrashing!

SMERALDINA. A man raise his hand to a woman? I'm shocked, sir, SHOCKED!

PANTALONE. *(Coming near her.)* Now don't you back-talk me, missy, or I'll

SMERALDINA. What, you'll chase me? You've always been too old to catch me before, why should now be any different? *(She exits, running.)*

PANTALONE. Minx! Saucy minx! Saucy minxy hussy minx! I'll show you I can chase —! Come back here! *(Runs after her.)*

TRUFFALDINO. *(Aside.)* Y'know, I haven't a clue how I'm gonna get out of this!

BEATRICE. *(Looking at the letter, aside.)* Poor Clarice! She despairs over Silvio's jealousy.

TRUFFALDINO. *(Tries to steal away quietly.)* I don't think this one's looking.

BEATRICE. Hey, where are you going?

TRUFFALDINO. Nowhere. *(Stops.)*

BEATRICE. Who is responsible for opening this letter?

TRUFFALDINO. I cannot tell a lie. It was Smeraldina.

BEATRICE. Smeraldina?! It was you, you lowlife half-wit! One and one make two, and that's the second letter of mine you've opened today. Come here.

TRUFFALDINO. *(Approaching timidly.)* Oh, sir, the quality of mercy is not strained —

BEATRICE. Come here, I say.

TRUFFALDINO. It falleth like the gentlest drop from heaven — *(Beatrice takes the stick which Truffaldino has at his flank — e.g., Harlequin's wooden sword or baton — and beats him well, standing with her back to the inn. Florindo appears at the window and sees the beating.)*

BEATRICE. Here's for the letters, here's for the check, and here's for the bad Shakespeare! (Throws stick on the ground, and exits. Florindo appears at a window of the inn.)*

FLORINDO. I say, what goes on here? Beating my servant? *(Leaves window.)*

TRUFFALDINO. The shame! Beaten like a drum! *(Florindo*

49

comes out.) It's an affront to you, sir, when you think about it.

FLORINDO. Who gave you that thrashing?

TRUFFALDINO. If only I knew, sir.

FLORINDO. Well, if you didn't know him, why did he thrash you?

TRUFFALDINO. Well, er —

FLORINDO. You let yourself be beaten and made no attempt to defend yourself? And in doing nothing, exposed your master to mockery, insult, and injury with all the consequences therein implied? *(Picks up the stick, beats him.)* This is for the mockery, this is for the insult, this is for the injury, and this is for all the consequences therein implied. *(Thrashes him and exit into inn.)*

TRUFFALDINO. Well, there's no doubt about it! I'm a servant of two masters 'cause they've both paid me twice the going rate! *(Exits into the inn.)*

Scene 2

A room in Brighella's inn. Truffaldino enters, shaking his shoulders and talking to himself.

TRUFFALDINO. They beat me, they beat me, they beat me … Frankly, I don't care if they beat me, long as they feed me, and tonight I'll be fed even better than this afternoon; and as long as I serve two masters, I'm a two-income family. Let's see now … Master Number One is out on business, Master Number Two is taking his nap. I think I'll give their clothes an airing — take them out of the trunks. Here are the keys, this room will do. *(Calls.)* Hey, waiters! *(Enter Waiters.)*

FIRST WAITER. What now?

TRUFFALDINO. Help me bring some trunks out of those rooms. I need to give the clothes some air.

FIRST WAITER. *(To Second Waiter.)* You help him.

TRUFFALDINO. *(To Second Waiter.)* Come on, what I get paid I'll give you half. *(Truffaldino and Second Waiter exit.)*

FIRST WAITER. Gotta admit: the guy's good — quick, eager, everything a servant should be. I don't trust him. I was a servant once myself, so I know the score. Nobody does nothin' just for the love of

it. Either he's robbing his master blind or he's throwin' dust in his eyes. *(Truffaldino reenters with the Second Waiter carrying a trunk.)*
TRUFFALDINO. Be careful! Put it down here. *(They put the trunk in the middle of the room.)* Now let's get the other, but quiet, my master is asleep. *(Truffaldino and Second Waiter exit in the opposite direction.)*
FIRST WAITER. Yeah, he's too good to be true. I never saw nobody wait on two masters the way this guy does. I'm gonna keep my eyes on him. Working for two masters at once is the easiest way to rob 'em both. *(Truffaldino and Second Waiter reenter with the other trunk.)*
TRUFFALDINO. Put this one here. *(They put it down a little way off from the other. To Second Waiter.)* There! You can go now.
FIRST WAITER. *(To Second Waiter.)* You heard him, go back to the kitchen. *(Exit Second Waiter. To Truffaldino.)* Need any further assistance?
TRUFFALDINO. No, thank you; I can handle this myself.
FIRST WAITER. A man who loves his work. More power to ya. *(Exit First Waiter.)*
TRUFFALDINO. At least I can do my work in peace and quiet, with no one to bother me. *(Takes a key out of his pocket.)* Now which key is this? Which trunk does it fit? Let's try this one. *(Opens one trunk.)* Right the first time! I'm a genius! Ergo this key will open the other trunk. *(Takes out second key and opens second trunk.)* Two for two! Let's empty 'em out. *(He takes all the clothes out of both trunks and puts them on the table. In each trunk there must be a black suit, books and papers, and anything else ad lib.)* See if there's anything in the pockets. You never know, sometimes they leave cookies or candy or meat pies — *(Searches the pockets of Beatrice's suit and finds a portrait.)* Ho, ho, ho, a little picture! Now that is a handsome man! Who can it be? Funny. Face is familiar, but I can't place it. He kinda looks like my other master. Except he's not wearing the right clothes, and that wig — *(Florindo calls from his room.)*
FLORINDO. *(Off.)* Truffaldino!
TRUFFALDINO. Damnation! He woke up. If he comes out and sees my other master's trunk, he'll want to know — quick, quick — I'll lock it up and say I don't know whose it is. *(Begins putting clothes in again.)*
FLORINDO. *(Off.)* Truffaldino!
TRUFFALDINO. Coming, sir! *(Aside.)* Gotta hide these first. But which coat goes with which trunk? And which trunk goes

with the book? Which trunk is which? Which coat is which? Which which is —

FLORINDO. *(Off.)* Do you want another beating?

TRUFFALDINO. In a minute, sir! *(Aside.)* I'll figure it out once he's gone! *(He stuffs the things into the trunks and locks them. Florindo enters in a dressing gown.)*

FLORINDO. What are you doing?

TRUFFALDINO. Well, you said to give your clothes an airing. I was just doing it.

FLORINDO. Uh-huh. And whose trunk is that?

TRUFFALDINO. Oh, that's your trunk sir.

FLORINDO. No, this trunk is mine. Give me my black coat.

TRUFFALDINO. Very good, sir. *(Opens Florindo's trunk and gives him the black suit. Florindo takes off his dressing gown with Truffaldino's help and puts on the black coat; then puts his hand into the pockets and finds the portrait.)*

FLORINDO. What's this?

TRUFFALDINO. *(Aside.)* Oh NO! I switched coats, that should be in my other master's pocket. Why do they all have to wear BLACK coats!

FLORINDO. *(Aside.)* There can be no mistake. This is my own portrait; the one I gave to my beloved Beatrice. *(To Truffaldino.)* Tell me, how did this portrait come to be in my coat pocket? It wasn't there before.

TRUFFALDINO. *(Aside.)* There's an answer to this. I don't know what it is, but there's an answer. *(Jumps in trunk, shuts it.)*

FLORINDO. *(Knocking on trunk.)* Truffaldino!

TRUFFALDINO. Who's there?

FLORINDO. A friend.

TRUFFALDINO. A friend who?

FLORINDO. Your master, Florindo Aretusi. *(He opens lid of trunk and pulls Truffaldino out.)*

TRUFFALDINO. *(Comes out of trunk with a pair of bloomers over his head.)* I can't see. God has struck me blind. *(Florindo removes bloomers.)* I see the light!

FLORINDO. Truffaldino! How did this portrait get in my pocket?

TRUFFALDINO. Sir, forgive me for taking advantage of my station. This portrait belongs to me. I hid it in your coat pocket because I was afraid I might lose it.

FLORINDO. How did you come by this portrait?

TRUFFALDINO. My master left it to me.

FLORINDO. Left it to you?

TRUFFALDINO. Yes, sir, he died and left me ... his portrait. We were very close.

FLORINDO. Alas, when did this master of yours die?

TRUFFALDINO. Uhhh, a week ago. *(Aside.)* It's like I'm channeling.

FLORINDO. What was your master's name?

TRUFFALDINO. I don't know. He was always in disguise.

FLORINDO. Incognito?

TRUFFALDINO. No, in Turin!

FLORINDO. How long did you work for him?

TRUFFALDINO. Week, week and a half.

FLORINDO. *(Aside.)* Beatrice! Alack! Couldst be she? Indeed she fled here as a man. Oh, unhappy me.

TRUFFALDINO. *(Aside.)* As he seems to be buying this, I might as well embroider.

FLORINDO. Tell me, was your master young?

TRUFFALDINO. Very young.

FLORINDO. Beardless?

TRUFFALDINO. Beardless.

FLORINDO. *(Aside.)* 'Tis she! Beloved, beardless Beatrice! *(To Truffaldino.)* Your young master from Turin is really dead?

TRUFFALDINO. Dead, dead, dead.

FLORINDO. From what did he die?

TRUFFALDINO. ... he had an accident.

FLORINDO. Where is he buried?

TRUFFALDINO. *(Aside.)* I didn't see that one coming. *(To Florindo.)* He wasn't buried, sir.

FLORINDO. What!

TRUFFALDINO. No, sir, his former servant came, put him in a coffin and mailed him back home.

FLORINDO. Was this the same servant who got you to pick up his letters from the post office?

TRUFFALDINO. Aye, sir. 'Twas ... Pasquale.

FLORINDO. *(Aside.)* All is lost. Beatrice is dead. Poor girl, the perils of the journey and the tortures of her heart must have killed her. Oh! I can no longer endure the agony of my grief! *(Exit to his room.)*

TRUFFALDINO. Gee, that portrait made him really emotional. My sorry tale must've stirred something deep inside his sympathetic soul. And yet I made the whole thing up so he wouldn't get wise to the trick with the trunks. The trunks! Gotta take them back to the rooms, or I'll get in more troub — Oop! It's the other master come to give me another piece of his mind. *(Enter Beatrice and Pantalone.)*

BEATRICE. I assure you, Signor Pantalone, the last shipment you sent me has been billed twice.

PANTALONE. Maybe the boys in the warehouse made a mistake. We'll go over my books again, and then we'll know where we stand.

BEATRICE. Well, luckily I have my own set of books to compare them to. One of us will owe the other. Truffaldino!

TRUFFALDINO. Sir!

BEATRICE. Where's the key to my trunk?

TRUFFALDINO. Right here, sir.

BEATRICE. What's my trunk doing in this room?

TRUFFALDINO. I was airing your clothes, sir.

BEATRICE. And have you aired them?

TRUFFALDINO. I have, sir.

BEATRICE. Then open the trunk and give me — wait, whose trunk is that?

TRUFFALDINO. Another gentleman who's just arrived.

BEATRICE. Give me my ledger book.

TRUFFALDINO. Yes, sir. *(Aside.)* Show me the way Lord! *(Opens trunk and looks for the book.)*

PANTALONE. As I say, if we've made a mistake; there'll be no charge.

BEATRICE. If everything's in order ...

TRUFFALDINO. Is this the book, sir? *(Holding out a book to Beatrice.)*

BEATRICE. I should think. There'll be no problem. *(Takes the book without looking carefully and opens it.)* Wait, this isn't my book! — Whose book is this?

TRUFFADINO. *(Stymied.)* ... Keep in touch. *(Jumps into trunk again.)*

BEATRICE. *(Aside.)* These are the two letters I wrote to Florindo! I tremble, I sweat, I know not where I am!

PANTALONE. Signor Federigo? Are you ill?

BEATRICE. It's nothing, Truffaldino. How did this book get in my trunk?

TRUFFALDINO. *(Inside trunk.)* I don't know, sir —

BEATRICE. *(Pulls him out.)* Out with the truth!

TRUFFALDINO. Sir, forgive me for taking advantage of my station. This book belongs to me. I hid it in your trunk because I was afraid I might lose it. *(Aside.)* It worked for one master, it'll work for the other.

BEATRICE. So you gave me your book instead of mine and didn't notice?

TRUFFALDINO. *(Aside.)* Obviously, he's the clever master. *(To Beatrice.)* Tell you the truth, sir; I only had the book a short time, I didn't recognize it at first.

BEATRICE. So how'd you get it?

TRUFFALDINO. My previous master here in Venice died and willed the book to me.

BEATRICE. How long ago?

TRUFFALDINO. Week, week and a half.

BEATRICE. But I met up with you in Verona.

TRUFFALDINO. Which is where I was having just come from Venice on account of my poor master's death.

BEATRICE. *(Aside.)* Alas! *(To Truffaldino.)* Your master — was his name — Florindo Aretusi?

TRUFFALDINO. Florindo Aretusi, as I live and breathe, even though he doesn't.

BEATRICE. And you're sure he's dead?

TRUFFALDINO. Dead, dead, dead.

BEATRICE. How did he die? Where is he buried?

TRUFFALDINO. He fell into a canal, sank like a stone and was never seen again.

BEATRICE. Oh, wretched me! Dead is Florindo! Dead is my love! Dead is my only hope! What purpose serves this, my useless life, when dies the one for whom I lived? All is lost. Love's twisted plots are but a heartless maze! I left my home, I left my family, I dressed in manly garb, I confronted danger, I hazarded my very life, all for Florindo —

PANTALONE. What an actress!

BEATRICE. I no longer bear the light of day. My adored one, my beloved, I follow you to thy tomb. *(Beatrice exits, weeping.)*

PANTALONE. *(Who has listened to her speech with astonishment.)* Truffaldino?

TRUFFALDINO. Sir?

PANTALONE. Did he say he was a woman?

TRUFFALDINO. A female woman!

PANTALONE. What a surprise!

TRUFFALDINO. What a plot twist!

PANTALONE. I'm speechless!

TRUFFALDINO. I'm clueless!

PANTALONE. I'm going home to tell my daughter. *(Exit.)*

TRUFFALDINO. So, I'm not a servant of two masters after all, I'm a servant of a master and a mistress. *(Exit.)*

Scene 3

A bridge over a canal — "water" below.

PANTALONE. My problems are solved, my worries are gone, our long national nightmare is over. Clarice can marry her beloved Silvio after all and lucky me here comes Silvio. *(Enter Silvio.)*
SILVIO. *(Aside.)* Ah-ha! Pantalone! My chance at last.
PANTALONE. Signor Silvio, I have good news, if you will hear it.
SILVIO. What say you, sir? Speak!
PANTALONE. The marriage of my daughter to Signor Federigo has foundered.
SILVIO. No! You deceive me!
PANTALONE. It's true. And if your affections have not been fickle, my daughter is prepared to render you her hand.
SILVIO. Zounds! I am recalled to Life! But wait! How can I clasp a hand that has so intimately clasped another's?
PANTALONE. Long story short: *(Muffeletta enters.)* Federigo Rasponi is Beatrice, his sister.
SILVIO. ... I don't get it.
PANTALONE. The gentleman we thought was Federigo is in fact Beatrice.
SILVIO. ... I don't get it.
PANTALONE. *(Aside.)* It's like talking to meat. *(To Silvio.)* Federigo is Beatrice dressed as a man.
SILVIO. Dressed as a man?
PANTALONE. Dressed as a man.
SILVIO. Dressed as a man ... Now I get it!
PANTALONE. And in record time.
SILVIO. But what happened?
PANTALONE. Go into my house. My daughter doesn't know any of this yet. I'll explain it to you both.
SILVIO. Yes, sir. And sir? Can you ever forgive me? Only a fool rides off on a horse called ... Stupid Dumb Horse —

PANTALONE. Come on, son-in-law, your bride-to-be awaits!

SILVIO. *(Aside.)* Canst find a fellow frothier? Canst find a heart more full?

PANTALONE. *(Ad-lib.)* Frothy boy, let's move it!

SILVIO. Feh! *(They exit with Muffeletta. Just then Beatrice and Florindo enter simultaneously; each holds a rope tied to a rock and is on the point of committing suicide. They both come forward in such a way that Beatrice and Florindo are unaware of each other's presence.)*

FLORINDO. I can no longer endure the agony of my grief.

BEATRICE. I can no longer bear the light of day. *(Bumps into Florindo, but doesn't see him.)* Excuse me.

FLORINDO. *(Equally blind.)* Sorry ... Beatrice, I will follow you to the grave!

BEATRICE. Florindo, I will jump into the wave. *(Florindo and Beatrice see each other, recognize each other, and stand dazed.)*

FLORINDO. Beatrice!

BEATRICE. Florindo!

FLORINDO. Who do I see?

BEATRICE. Florindo!

FLORINDO. Beatrice!

BEATRICE. Alive?

FLORINDO. You too?

BEATRICE. Oh, joy!

FLORINDO. Oh, rapture! *(They drop their rocks into the "water" and are almost pulled into the canal by the ropes. They struggle to save each other ... and do.)* Why were you going to do away with yourself?

BEATRICE. Because of the news of your premature death.

FLORINDO. Who said I was dead?

BEATRICE. My servant.

FLORINDO. My servant told me YOU too had fled this vale of tears. The grief was too much to bear, and so I threw my rock to drown myself. We must seek our servants out and confront their villainy. *(Brighella enters.)* Hey, you, Brighella!

BRIGHELLA. You bellowed manfully, sir?

FLORINDO. Where are our servants?

BRIGHELLA. I don't know. You want I should look?

FLORINDO. At once. And send them to us pronto!

BRIGHELLA. I only know the one, but lemme check with the waiters, they worked with 'em both. Oh, and by the way, loved your death scene, but in the future, double suicides are bad for business. *(Exit Brighella.)*

FLORINDO. Tell me: your brother Federigo — is he dead?

BEATRICE. He died on the spot.

FLORINDO. But I was told he was alive and well and here in Venice.

BEATRICE. No. That was me.

FLORINDO. My dear, what shall we do about your flight from Turin?

BEATRICE. If I go back as your wife with you as my husband, all will be made right again.

FLORINDO. I am charged with your brother's death. The toll of justice won't be deafened by the ringing of wedding bells.

BEATRICE. No, but they may be by the tinkle of coins. Once I've collected the money Pantalone owed Federigo, we'll buy your freedom.

FLORINDO. Ah, justice! But, where are those two servants of ours? Here comes one. *(Enter Truffaldino, brought in by force by Brighella and the First Waiter.)* Don't be scared. We mean you no harm. Right?

BEATRICE. Yes … we come in peace.

TRUFFALDINO. *(Aside.)* Yeah, they came in peace when they beat me with a stick.

BRIGHELLA. We caught this one close by. We find his pal, we'll bring him right away.

FLORINDO. Yes, I want the both of them here together! *(First Waiter and Brighella exit.)* All right, the truth: How did the portrait and the book get into our belongings?

BEATRICE. Why did you conspire to drive us crazy?

TRUFFALDINO. *(To Florindo.)* Sir? May I have a word with you in private? *(To Beatrice, just as he turns to speak to Florindo.)* Hold that thought.

FLORINDO. Beg pardon, my little chocolate blossom.

TRUFFALDINO. *(To Florindo.)* Master, I am innocent of all charges. The guilty party is Pasquale, the servant of that lady there. *(Pointing at Beatrice.)* He switched the stuff in the trunk and the pockets of the coat and pleaded with me to take the blame, because he was afraid his master would fire him, and well, I guess I'm just a sentimental softie who'd lay down his life at the drop of a hat, so I made up all those stories to help him, never dreaming it was a portrait of you or that you'd get so angry about the death of that other person. Now that I've come clean, I'm sure you'll see that I am indeed an honest and faithful servant.

BEATRICE. Is there an intermission in this story? 'Cause I'd like to know what's going on here.

FLORINDO. Then the fellow who got you to fetch that letter from the post office was the servant of Signora Beatrice?

TRUFFALDINO. Yes, sir, Pasquale, sir, he's who done it, sir.

FLORINDO. You and Pasquale both deserve a beating.

TRUFFALDINO. (Aside.) And I'll bet we both get one.

BEATRICE. I hate to interrupt, but have you two finished?

FLORINDO. This fellow has been telling me —

TRUFFALDINO. (To Florindo.) Sir! Don't let on you know about Pasquale! Tell the lady it was me! Punish me! Beat me! But don't mention Pasquale.

FLORINDO. (To Truffaldino.) You must really love this Pasquale, huh?

TRUFFALDINO. Like my own self! Now I will confess to the lady. She can yell at me, she can whip me, she can have her way with me, but never will I finger Pasquale!

FLORINDO. Yes, well, we certainly wouldn't want you to finger — to do that.

TRUFFALDINO. Madam?

BEATRICE. Finished so soon? Dare I ask you to repeat it?

TRUFFALDINO. You remember I told you about that gentleman's servant? Well! (Very fast.) The guilty party is Pasquale, the servant of that gentleman there. (Pointing at Florindo.) He switched the stuff in the trunk and the pockets of the coat and pleaded with me to take the blame, because he was afraid his master would fire him, and well, I guess I'm just a sentimental softie who'd lay down his life at the drop of a hat, so I made up all those stories to help him, never dreaming it was a portrait of you or that you'd get so angry about the death of that other person. Now that I've come clean, I'm sure you'll see that I am indeed an honest and faithful servant.

FLORINDO. All right, time's up. Signora Beatrice, I know both our servants deserve to be punished; but given the fact that the two of us have been blessed with a happy ending, I think we should forgive these errant knaves and give them a happy ending too.

BEATRICE. But your servant —

TRUFFALDINO. (Aside to Beatrice.) Madam! Don't mention Pasquale!

BEATRICE. All right! I'm going to go to Signor Pantalone's. Will you escort me?

FLORINDO. There's nothing in the world I'd rather do, but I

have an appointment with my banker.

BEATRICE. I won't budge 'til I see your fast-approaching form.

FLORINDO. You're not going to change?

BEATRICE. You don't like my outfit?

FLORINDO. I'd like you better without pants — er, I mean, I should far prefer your beauty be not so thoroughly ... encased.

BEATRICE. Uh-huh. See you at Pantalone's. Truffaldino knows the way. *(Exit Beatrice.)*

TRUFFALDINO. Well, he wasn't here! His master wanted to dress, and he's nowhere to be found!

FLORINDO. Hmm. Help me dress.

TRUFFALDINO. Yes sir, and then we go to Signor Pantalone's?

FLORINDO. Yes, why?

TRUFFALDINO. I want to ask a favor.

FLORINDO. After all you've done?

TRUFFALDINO. You realize that if there have been any minor problems here or there, it's Pasquale we have to blame?

FLORINDO. Yes, yes, but where is this Pasquale? Can't we at least see him?

TRUFFALDINO. Oh, he'll show eventually. But the favor I wanted to ask ... well, you see, sir, I'm in love too.

FLORINDO. ... In love?

TRUFFALDINO. With a young woman who is the maid to Signor Pantalone; and seeing that I'm your servant and you're my master, maybe you could put in a good word for me.

FLORINDO. Does the girl want you?

TRUFFALDINO. Who wouldn't! All I need is for you to vouch for me.

FLORINDO. It'll be a pleasure. But how can you afford to have a wife?

TRUFFALDINO. I'll get by ... with a little help from Pasquale.

FLORINDO. Fine by me, but if I were you, I'd rely on someone with a bit more sense. *(Florindo exits.)*

TRUFFALDINO. If I don't show some sense now, I never will. *(Exits.)*

Scene 4

A room in the house of Pantalone. Clarice enters, pouting. Pantalone, Silvio, Dr. Lombardi and Smeraldina follow and try to assuage her.

PANTALONE. Clarice, you're being very difficult! Silvio admits he went a little over the top, but see how sorry he is? So he behaved like a fool, so he sat on his butt while you tried to kill yourself ... that's how men show love!

SILVIO. Your father's right, Clarice. I'm really the victim here. I know I hurt you, but take your own pain and multiply it by a very large number, and that's how much pain I was in.

DR. LOMBARDI. Verily, my dear presumptive daughter-in-law, have pity on my idiot son; his brain is small and seldom used.

SMERALDINA. It's up to you. Granted, men are pigs. Granted, they're hypocrites. Granted, they treat us like dirt and beat us like rugs ... and yes, there's a "but" coming — but love is our sickness, madam, and man is the only medicine. Think of him as something bad you swallow today to make you better tomorrow.

PANTALONE. Smeraldina's right. Drink up, Silvio's not rat poison.

DR. LOMBARDI. Verily, Silvio is not rat poison, nor is he even very unpleasant anti-vermin medicine as medicine goes.

SILVIO. Clarice, say something! I know I deserve to be punished but, punish me with words, not silence.

CLARICE. *(To Silvio.)* Bastard.

PANTALONE. She spoke!

DR. LOMBARDI. 'Tis a sign!

SMERALDINA. We got momentum on their side now.

SILVIO. If you desire my blood to avenge my cruelty, I will give it from the pumphouse of my heart. But, if, on the other hand, instead of the blood in my veins, you would accept that other bodily fluid which gushes from my eyes — ! *(Weeps.)*

PANTALONE. Bravo!

CLARICE. *(Giving in.)* Bastard.

PANTALONE. Brava!

DR. LOMBARDI. We're almost there ...

PANTALONE. Here. *(Takes Silvio and Clarice's hands.)* Now, join your hands together again and make peace.

SILVIO. *(Pleading.)* Oh, Signora Clarice!

CLARICE. *(Yielding more.)* Pig!

SILVIO. Petal!

CLARICE. *(More.)* Beast!

SILVIO. Beloved!

CLARICE. *(More.)* Monster!

SILVIO. Snickerdoodle of my soul!

CLARICE. *(Gives in entirely.)* ... Oh, okay!

PANTALONE. Going, going —

CLARICE. I forgive you.

ALL. Gone! *(Enter Brighella.)*

BRIGHELLA. 'Scuse me, sir, may I come in?

PANTALONE. Please do, Brighella. After all, it was you who told me about Signor Federigo, eh?

BRIGHELLA. Oh, sir ... who would NOT have been deceived? Twins, brother and sister, peas, pods.

PANTALONE. Yeah, okay, enough. What do you want?

BRIGHELLA. Signora Beatrice is here, and wants you should receive her.

PANTALONE. So show her in. *(Enter Beatrice in a stunning gown.)*

BEATRICE. Ladies and gentlemen, I come to ask your pardon and forgiveness, that you should on my account have been put to such woe and heartache.

CLARICE. Oh, YOU! Hug! *(Embraces her.)*

SILVIO. *(Annoyed at the embrace.)* Uh — what's all this?

BEATRICE. Haven't you ever seen two sisters embrace one another?

SILVIO. *(Dense as ever.)* You're sisters?

BEATRICE. No, I mean —

CLARICE. Leave it.

SILVIO. Oh, who cares?! I want all the world to be happy! Let's all get married!

SMERALDINA. What about me?

SILVIO. Who are you going to marry?

SMERALDINA. The first man that comes along. *(Enter Truffaldino.)*

TRUFFALDINO. Did I hear my name?

BEATRICE. Where is Signor Florindo?

TRUFFALDINO. He's ready and waiting and eager to enter.

BEATRICE. Signor Pantalone, will you welcome Florindo?

PANTALONE. Is that your young gentleman?
BEATRICE. He is my fiancé.
PANTALONE. I would be honored.
BEATRICE. Show him in.
TRUFFALDINO. *(To Smeraldina.)* Why, madam! Fancy meeting you here!
SMERALDINA. Nice to see you too, swarthy one.
TRUFFALDINO. We need to straighten a few things out.
SMERALDINA. What about?
TRUFFALDINO. *(Makes as though giving her a wedding ring.)* Watch me.
SMERALDINA. *(Ecstatic.)* A ring? You? Me? Marriage! Oh boy!
BEATRICE. *(Impatient.)* Uhhh ...
TRUFFALDINO. We'll talk. *(Exits.)*
SMERALDINA. Signora Clarice, may I speak with you?
CLARICE. What is it?
SMERALDINA. That dark, hairy boy is the servant of Signora Beatrice. He wants to marry me, and if you could drop a word in his mistress's ear...?
CLARICE. I will do so at the earliest possible convenience. *(Truffaldino and Florindo enter.)*
FLORINDO. Sir, I present myself at the behest of Signora Beatrice. Signora Beatrice is to be my wife, and we'd like you to give away the bride.
PANTALONE. Oh, we're all going to live happily ever after!
TRUFFALDINO. *(To Florindo.)* Sir? A word.
FLORINDO. What now?
TRUFFALDINO. You remember you promised to ask Signor Pantalone for Smeraldina as my wife...? I want a happy ending too, you know.
FLORINDO. Signor Pantalone, although this is the first occasion on which I have had the honor of knowing you, I fear I must be bold in asking you a favor. My servant desires to marry your maid.
PANTALONE. Is this servant of yours a good honest man?
FLORINDO. He's only been with me a day, but so far he has proved himself trustworthy and intermittently intelligent.
CLARICE. Signor Florindo, you have beat me to the punch! I was supposed to propose marriage between my maid and the servant of Signora Beatrice. But seeing that you've requested her hand for your servant, I guess there's nothing I can do about it.
FLORINDO. No, please, you precede me, after you.

63

CLARICE. No, no. I pray sir, please continue.

FLORINDO. No, no, I will not say another word on behalf of my servant. In fact, I will actively oppose my servant marrying your maid.

CLARICE. Sir, if your man doesn't marry her, then no man shall marry her.

TRUFFALDINO. *(Aside.)* Do you believe this? They're playing patty-cake, and I'm standing here without a wife!

SMERALDINA. *(Aside.)* How did I just get two proposals and no husband?

PANTALONE. Come on, the poor girl wants to get married, give her one of 'em!

FLORINDO. Nothing shall induce me to insult Signora Clarice!

CLARICE. Never will I tolerate an injustice to Signor Florindo.

TRUFFALDINO. Sir? Madam? Let me see if I can finesse this one. Signor Florindo, did you not request the hand of Smeraldina for your servant?

FLORINDO. Yes.

TRUFFALDINO. And you, Signora Clarice, did you not intend Smeraldina to marry the servant of Signora Beatrice?

CLARICE. Yes.

TRUFFALDINO. Gimme your hand, Smeraldina.

PANTALONE. What right have you to ask for her hand?

TRUFFALDINO. Because I am the servant of Signor Florindo AND Signora Beatrice.

FLORINDO. What?

BEATRICE. What'd he say?

FLORINDO. Signora Beatrice, where is your servant?

BEATRICE. Right here! Truffaldino!

FLORINDO. But Truffaldino is my servant!

BEATRICE. I thought your servant was called Pasquale!

FLORINDO. I thought your servant was called Pasquale!

BEATRICE. *(To Truffaldino.)* How do you explain this? *(Truffaldino makes silent gestures asking forgiveness from God.)*

FLORINDO. You cheeky rascal!

BEATRICE. You monkey!

FLORINDO. You waited on two masters at once? *(They all start to chase after Truffaldino. He runs around the stage, in the house. Actors run around, ad-libs. Someone brings one of the trunks onstage. Truffaldino jumps into the trunk and shuts it. When it is opened, there is no one in the trunk, just a red rose. Beatrice picks up the rose. Truffaldino appears above the stage.)*

64

TRUFFALDINO.
"The world revolves, first fast, then faster
'Til love doth make it pause.
The wisest hearts will know disaster
Say Cupid is the cause.
No more a servant of two masters
I serve to win applause."
(The actor who plays Truffaldino dies. The company looks at him. The actress who plays Beatrice picks up the red rose and gazes at him.)

End of Play

PROPERTY LIST

Duck or chicken on a leash (YOUNG WOMAN)
Instrument (MUSICIAN)
Handkerchief (TRUFFALDINO)
Satchel with bottle of medicine (PATRON)
Gold coin (PATRON)
Makeup (TRUFFALDINO)
Flower, mask (TRUFFALDINO)
Letters, coins (BEATRICE)
Sword (SILVIO)
Mint candy (SMERALDINA)
"Exposition" sign (GIRL)
Trunk (PORTER)
Coins (FLORINDO)
Letters (TRUFFALDINO)
Bread (TRUFFALDINO)
Sword (BEATRICE)
Note (PROMPTER)
Purse and keys (FLORINDO)
Check (BEATRICE)
Glasses, wine, bread (WAITERS)
Soup tureen, spoon (TRUFFALDINO, FIRST WAITER)
Dish of meat (FIRST WAITER, SECOND WAITER)
Dirty plates (TRUFFALDINO)
Plate of meatballs (SECOND WAITER)
Pudding (FIRST WAITER, TRUFFALDINO)
Trays (TRUFFALDINO)
Dish of duck (FIRST WAITER)
Dishes of food (FIRST and SECOND WAITERS)
Leg of chicken, feather (STAGEHAND)
Bottle, glass, napkin (TRUFFALDINO)
Letter (SMERALDINA)
Stick (TRUFFALDINO)
Two trunks with matching black suits, books and papers (TRUF-
     FALDINO and SECOND WAITER)
Key (TRUFFALDINO)
Rocks tied to ropes (BEATRICE and FLORINDO)
Trunk with red rose (TRUFFALDINO)

SOUND EFFECTS

Fanfare
Three loud bangs
Knock

NEW PLAMS

★ **THE GREAT AMERICAN TRAILER PARK MUSICAL music and lyrics by David Nehls, book by Betsy Kelso.** Pippi, a stripper on the run, has just moved into Armadillo Acres, wreaking havoc among the tenants of Florida's most exclusive trailer park. "Adultery, strippers, murderous ex-boyfriends, Costco and the Ice Capades. Undeniable fun." *–NY Post.* "Joyful and unashamedly vulgar." *–The New Yorker.* "Sparkles with treasure." *–New York Sun.* [2M, 5W] ISBN: 978-0-8222-2137-1

★ **MATCH by Stephen Belber.** When a young Seattle couple meet a prominent New York choreographer, they are led on a fraught journey that will change their lives forever. "Uproariously funny, deeply moving, enthralling theatre." *–NY Daily News.* "Prolific laughs and ear-to-ear smiles." *–NY Magazine.* [2M, 1W] ISBN: 978-0-8222-2020-6

★ **MR. MARMALADE by Noah Haidle.** Four-year-old Lucy's imaginary friend, Mr. Marmalade, doesn't have much time for her—not to mention he has a cocaine addiction and a penchant for pornography. "Alternately hilarious and heartbreaking." *–The New Yorker.* "A mature and accomplished play." *–LA Times.* "Scathingly observant comedy." *–Miami Herald.* [4M, 2W] ISBN: 978-0-8222-2142-5

★ **MOONLIGHT AND MAGNOLIAS by Ron Hutchinson.** Three men cloister themselves as they work tirelessly to reshape a screenplay that's just not working—*Gone with the Wind.* "Consumers of vintage Hollywood insider stories will eat up Hutchinson's diverting conjecture." *–Variety.* "A lot of fun." *–NY Post.* "A Hollywood dream-factory farce." *–Chicago Sun-Times.* [3M, 1W] ISBN: 978-0-8222-2084-8

★ **THE LEARNED LADIES OF PARK AVENUE by David Grimm, translated and freely adapted from Molière's *Les Femmes Savantes.*** Dicky wants to marry Betty, but her mother's plan is for Betty to wed a most pompous man. "A brave, brainy and barmy revision." *–Hartford Courant.* "A rare but welcome bird in contemporary theatre." *–New Haven Register.* "Roll over Cole Porter." *–Boston Globe.* [5M, 5W] ISBN: 978-0-8222-2135-7

★ **REGRETS ONLY by Paul Rudnick.** A sparkling comedy of Manhattan manners that explores the latest topics in marriage, friendships and squandered riches. "One of the funniest quip-meisters on the planet." *–NY Times.* "Precious moments of hilarity. Devastatingly accurate political and social satire." *–BackStage.* "Great fun." *–CurtainUp.* [3M, 3W] ISBN: 978-0-8222-2223-1

DRAMATISTS PLAY SERVICE, INC.
440 Park Avenue South, New York, NY 10016 212-683-8960 Fax 212-213-1539
postmaster@dramatists.com www.dramatists.com

NEW PLAYS

★ **AFTER ASHLEY by Gina Gionfriddo.** A teenager is unwillingly thrust into the national spotlight when a family tragedy becomes talk-show fodder. "A work that virtually any audience would find accessible." –*NY Times.* "Deft characterization and caustic humor." –*NY Sun.* "A smart satirical drama." –*Variety.* [4M, 2W] ISBN: 978-0-8222-2099-2

★ **THE RUBY SUNRISE by Rinne Groff.** Twenty-five years after Ruby struggles to realize her dream of inventing the first television, her daughter faces similar battles of faith as she works to get Ruby's story told on network TV. "Measured and intelligent, optimistic yet clear-eyed." –*NY Magazine.* "Maintains an exciting sense of ingenuity." –*Village Voice.* "Sinuous theatrical flair." –*Broadway.com.* [3M, 4W] ISBN: 978-0-8222-2140-1

★ **MY NAME IS RACHEL CORRIE taken from the writings of Rachel Corrie, edited by Alan Rickman and Katharine Viner.** This solo piece tells the story of Rachel Corrie who was killed in Gaza by an Israeli bulldozer set to demolish a Palestinian home. "Heartbreaking urgency. An invigoratingly detailed portrait of a passionate idealist." –*NY Times.* "Deeply authentically human." –*USA Today.* "A stunning dramatization." –*CurtainUp.* [1W] ISBN: 978-0-8222-2222-4

★ **ALMOST, MAINE by John Cariani.** This charming midwinter night's dream of a play turns romantic clichés on their ear as it chronicles the painfully hilarious amorous adventures (and misadventures) of residents of a remote northern town that doesn't quite exist. "A whimsical approach to the joys and perils of romance." –*NY Times.* "Sweet, poignant and witty." –*NY Daily News.* "Aims for the heart by way of the funny bone." –*Star-Ledger.* [2M, 2W] ISBN: 978-0-8222-2156-2

★ **Mitch Albom's TUESDAYS WITH MORRIE by Jeffrey Hatcher and Mitch Albom, based on the book by Mitch Albom.** The true story of Brandeis University professor Morrie Schwartz and his relationship with his student Mitch Albom. "A touching, life affirming, deeply emotional drama." –*NY Daily News.* "You'll laugh. You'll cry." –*Variety.* "Moving and powerful." –*NY Post.* [2M] ISBN: 978-0-8222-2188-3

★ **DOG SEES GOD: CONFESSIONS OF A TEENAGE BLOCKHEAD by Bert V. Royal.** An abused pianist and a pyromaniac ex-girlfriend contribute to the teen-angst of America's most hapless kid. "A welcome antidote to the notion that the *Peanuts* gang provides merely American cuteness." –*NY Times.* "Hysterically funny." –*NY Post.* "The *Peanuts* kids have finally come out of their shells." –*Time Out.* [4M, 4W] ISBN: 978-0-8222-2152-4

DRAMATISTS PLAY SERVICE, INC.
440 Park Avenue South, New York, NY 10016 212-683-8960 Fax 212-213-1539
postmaster@dramatists.com   www.dramatists.com

NEW PLAGS

★ **RABBIT HOLE by David Lindsay-Abaire.** Winner of the 2007 Pulitzer Prize. Becca and Howie Corbett have everything a couple could want until a life-shattering accident turns their world upside down. "An intensely emotional examination of grief, laced with wit." *–Variety.* "A transcendent and deeply affecting new play." *–Entertainment Weekly.* "Painstakingly beautiful." *–BackStage.* [2M, 3W] ISBN: 978-0-8222-2154-8

★ **DOUBT, A Parable by John Patrick Shanley.** Winner of the 2005 Pulitzer Prize and Tony Award. Sister Aloysius, a Bronx school principal, takes matters into her own hands when she suspects the young Father Flynn of improper relations with one of the male students. "All the elements come invigoratingly together like clockwork." *–Variety.* "Passionate, exquisite, important, engrossing." *–NY Newsday.* [1M, 3W] ISBN: 978-0-8222-2219-4

★ **THE PILLOWMAN by Martin McDonagh.** In an unnamed totalitarian state, an author of horrific children's stories discovers that someone has been making his stories come true. "A blindingly bright black comedy." *–NY Times.* "McDonagh's least forgiving, bravest play." *–Variety.* "Thoroughly startling and genuinely intimidating." *–Chicago Tribune.* [4M, 5 bit parts (2M, 1W, 1 boy, 1 girl)] ISBN: 978-0-8222-2100-5

★ **GREY GARDENS book by Doug Wright, music by Scott Frankel, lyrics by Michael Korie.** The hilarious and heartbreaking story of Big Edie and Little Edie Bouvier Beale, the eccentric aunt and cousin of Jacqueline Kennedy Onassis, once bright names on the social register who became East Hampton's most notorious recluses. "An experience no passionate theatergoer should miss." *–NY Times.* "A unique and unmissable musical." *–Rolling Stone.* [4M, 3W, 2 girls] ISBN: 978-0-8222-2181-4

★ **THE LITTLE DOG LAUGHED by Douglas Carter Beane.** Mitchell Green could make it big as the hot new leading man in Hollywood if Diane, his agent, could just keep him in the closet. "Devastatingly funny." *–NY Times.* "An out-and-out delight." *–NY Daily News.* "Full of wit and wisdom." *–NY Post.* [2M, 2W] ISBN: 978-0-8222-2226-2

★ **SHINING CITY by Conor McPherson.** A guilt-ridden man reaches out to a therapist after seeing the ghost of his recently deceased wife. "Haunting, inspired and glorious." *–NY Times.* "Simply breathtaking and astonishing." *–Time Out.* "A thoughtful, artful, absorbing new drama." *–Star-Ledger.* [3M, 1W] ISBN: 978-0-8222-2187-6

DRAMATISTS PLAY SERVICE, INC.
440 Park Avenue South, New York, NY 10016 212-683-8960 Fax 212-213-1539
postmaster@dramatists.com   www.dramatists.com